ACCIDENTS IN NORTH AMERICAN MOUNTAINEERING

VOLUME 9 • NUMBER 1 • ISSUE 59
2006

THE AMERICAN ALPINE CLUB
GOLDEN

THE ALPINE CLUB OF CANADA
BANFF

ISSN   0065-082X
ISBN   1-933056-02-9
Manufactured in the United States

Published by
The American Alpine Club, Inc.
710 Tenth Street, Suite 100
Golden, CO 80401

Cover Illustrations
Front: Fred Wilkinson assisting an injured climber who is being lowered in a single 400-foot lower from the top of Standard Route, Frankenstein Cliff, New Hampshire. The injured climber broke both ankles in a 15-foot fall when both tools popped out on the finishing moves of the climb. Photograph by Al Hospers.
Back: Why helmets are a good idea. This one saved Scott McGee when he was hit by rockfall on The Snaz. (See Wyoming, July 24.) Photograph by Scott McGee.

♲ Printed on recycled paper

CONTENTS

SAFETY COMMITTEES 2005

The American Alpine Club
Aram Attarian, John Dill, Mike Gauthier, Renny Jackson,
Daryl Miller, Jeff Sheetz, and John E. (Jed) Williamson (Chair)

The Alpine Club of Canada
Peter Amann (Jasper), Rob Chisnall (Kingston), Dave McCormick
(Chair), Scott McLarty (Calgary), Frank Pianka (Thunder Bay)
Selina Swets (Vancouver)

ACCIDENTS IN
NORTH AMERICAN MOUNTAINEERING
Fifty-Ninth Annual Report of the Safety Committees
of The American Alpine Club and The Alpine Club of Canada

This is the fifty-ninth issue of *Accidents in North American Mountaineering* and the twenty-eighth issue in which The Alpine Club of Canada has contributed data and narratives.

Canada: In 2005 an unprecedented summer avalanche warning was issued for alpine climbing routes. Several avalanches were triggered in late June and early July with a large number of natural slides. Heavy snowfall, along with heavy rain in June, created a rain-soaked snowpack covered by a thin crust at higher elevations. Cooler weather, with dry snow and strong winds, formed a winter-type slab on top of crust on some slopes. The conditions were unusual for the time of year (being one month behind) and did not particularly improve through the season. Many climbers stayed away from their intended routes as a result.

It is difficult to obtain data from climbing areas in Canada outside of the Canadian Rockies. Park authorities provide information on a voluntary and non-funded basis. We thank wardens in Banff, Jasper, Yoho, and Waterton National Parks for participating in this endeavour. We also thank conservation officers in Kananaskis Country and Peter Lougheed Provincial Park in Alberta.

There were accidents we heard about but were not able to obtain sufficient details to include them in the summary. We rarely get reports from climbing areas east of Alberta and wish to encourage individuals or organizations in the eastern Provinces to contact us in future with any details which they can provide for local climbing areas.

We wish to thank the following individuals for their contributions and assistance in tracking down information throughout the year: Burke Duncan, Jeff Hunston, Garth Lemke and Dave Stephens.

United States: It seems that during this past year the trend of rappelling off the end of one's rope or having the anchor fail on the rappel set up and having the belay rope go through the belay device during lowering continued. Rappelling off the end incidents were the result of ropes being of unequal lengths, no knot in the ends (though as will be discussed, this practice is not always warranted), failure of the autoblock, or a combination of these.

In this issue, a few incidents are described at some length. Of particular note are the first two found in the Alaska section, the self-report on the first incident found in the Oregon section, and two incidents in Wyoming, one involving a climber rappelling from the end of his rope and one involving a climber who fell to her death while on descent. All were very experienced, which makes the lessons to be learned even more poignant. The Wyoming case has probably one of the most detailed analysis sections we've ever published. If the level of detail found here were included for each incident, this would be a much larger volume. One purpose for doing this is to illustrate that there is often more to be learned than can be found just in the facts of the case. A few of our correspondents often seek answers beyond the obvious. Look closely at the reports from Denali, Yosemite, and Rainier National Parks to see good examples from previous years.

Michelle Schonzeit, who has been working for the National Park Service, continued working with us this year. She took on the job of analyzing incidents from the State of Colorado. She compiled the data and had completed the narratives when her computer went down. The data had made it to hardcopy, fortunately, but the reports did not, as noted in that section.

As always, we seek help from the climbing corners of the country. It remains apparent that we are not getting reports from such centers as Joshua Tree National Park, Baraboo State Park, and the Smokey Mountain National Park, to name but a few. It is encouraging to hear from some places, like City of Rocks, that there are no significant accidents to report! That information is just as valuable.

On October 26–29, the Wilderness Risk Manager Conference will be held in Killington, Vermont. (Go to www.NOLS.org for information on the program and registration.)

In addition to the dedicated individuals on the Safety Committee, we are grateful to the following—with apologies for any omissions—for collecting data and for helping with the report: Hank Alacandri, Dave Brown, Ned Houston, Erik Hansen, Al Hospers, Scott McGee, Tom Moyer, Leo Paik, Michelle Schonzeit, Robert Speik, Eric White, all individuals who sent in personal stories, and, of course, George Sainsbury.

John E. (Jed) Williamson
Managing Editor
7 River Ridge Road
Hanover, NH 03755
e-mail: jedwmsn@sover.net

Edwina Podemski
Canadian Editor
700 Phipps McKinnon Building
10020-101A Avenue
Edmonton, Alberta T5J 3G2
e-mail: cwep@compusmart.ab.ca

CANADA

RAPPEL ERROR—MISUSE OF GRIGRI
Baffin Island, Stewart Valley

On April 24, Drew Wilson, Kyle Dempster, Grover Shipman, Ross Cowan, and I (Pete Dronkers) left Ottawa for Baffin Island to make a first ascent in Stewart Valley. I knew of only four routes there, two of which were professionally organized expeditions to Great Sail Peak.

We left Clyde River in sub-zero temperatures and made the first sledged crossing from Sam Ford Fjord to Stewart Valley, establishing camp beneath Great Sail Peak. We knew of no other climbers in northeastern Baffin.

We chose a 2,200-foot overhanging spire south of Great Sail Peak and moved camp to the unnamed tower. Dempster (22) and Wilson (24) began fixing up snow and rock slabs while Cowan (41) and Shipman (32) and I (25) brought loads up the 2,000-foot approach.

Wilson and Dempster continued fixing—mostly free—over loose rock above a hanging snowfield, and Shipman and I narrowly avoided being hit. Wilson completed the free crux at 5.11—a traverse on loose flakes. Shipman would remain in base camp while we climbed in teams of two in shifts around the clock. While sorting 18 days of food at base camp, Cowan declared that he was too overwhelmed to participate.

After the final hauls, we drilled our camp below a dihedral. We had pulled up 1,100 feet of rope from below, and were suspended 400 feet up overhanging rock. Lacking spotting scopes beforehand, route finding was achieved by jumping out from fixed lines. We climbed 60- and 70-meter pitches—which were generally continuous and thin—in extreme cold over many days. Dempster and Wilson—cousins with a long climbing partnership—accomplished most of the leads, as Cowan had intended to be my partner. Wilson accomplished the aid crux, an A4- hook traverse, and Dempster led an 80-meter pitch by tying ropes together.

With a thousand feet of rope fixed above, it appeared that the high point was within 600 feet of the summit, so we didn't move camp higher. By our tenth day on the wall, we could fix no more and so packed for a summit push, unaware if it was day or night.

It was snowing lightly as we left camp in poor visibility. Dempster excavated snow and ice from wide cracks above the high point. Finally, the angle eased and Wilson quickly drilled up a blank slab to gain a corner. Then we noticed the first blue skies after a week in poor weather. The clouds sank, revealing the most impressive view imaginable.

I aided to a pendulum point, then Wilson began free climbing with rock shoes, using bare fingertips in snow-filled 5.10 cracks. He continued up an overhanging bowl and arrived at a ledge ten feet from the summit. It had been 25 hours. We rested and talked in the warm sun, gazing over distant summits protruding from the massive ice caps beyond Stewart Valley.

Wilson and Dempster displayed their summit costumes—Dempster with hula skirt, and Wilson with an inflatable monkey. We had succeeded in the most significant climb of our lives. We began rappelling and collecting hardware and ropes. We slept well that day. Fourteen hours later, we had a casual breakfast in long sleeve shirts. Days before, Cowan and Shipman moved camp 3.5 miles towards Sam Ford Fjord, but would meet us below the wall to help us bring loads to the new camp. Soon our haulbags were packed and I jumared to retrieve two remaining ropes from above while Dempster and Wilson arranged the lowering system.

Wilson had fixed a 300-foot line with a 15-foot tail end to safeguard himself while maneuvering around the anchors. He was clipped to it with a Grigri. Another rope was needed to reach the snowfield, so he clipped a spare cord to his harness. He didn't tie knots in either end of the 300-foot rope.

Wilson would rappel first, then Dempster would lower the bags. I would descend last with the remaining ropes. Wilson must have forgotten that he was on the short end when he weighted the Grigri. He was speaking to Dempster as he began rappelling. It was the last time he was seen alive.

From above, I heard Wilson's scream. I looked down to see him falling through space, impacting hundreds of feet below, and finally coming to rest 700 feet below.

I descended to Dempster. There was enough rope to reach Wilson, so he rappelled to be sure there was no pulse. He wanted to lower all the bags immediately, so he returned to the anchors to set up a lowering system. I descended to the snowfield to dock the bags and dodged the rocks they dislodged. Fifteen hours after waking, everything was near Wilson's body.

I drilled an anchor where Wilson rested, retrieved my personal haulbag and continued rappelling. Dempster found a way to walk down, and met Cowan and Shipman to explain what happened. Later, we all decided to return to base camp and come back later to retrieve Wilson.

Temperatures on the lake had turned Styrofoam snow to wet slush. We post-holed to our knees with feet in ice water. The three-mile walk took five hours. At camp Shipman notified the police using our satellite phone. We agreed to retrieve Wilson after resting.

When we returned, Shipman and Dempster prepared Wilson for lowering using a long plastic sled. Soon everything was at lake level, but because it required all of our collective strength to push Wilson, we could carry nothing else. It was raining, and the slush was waist deep in places. We left the bags tied together in case a helicopter could retrieve them. We returned to camp exhausted and received confirmation that the police had been dispatched to Sam Ford Fjord—about three miles away—to aid in the extraction of the body.

An outfitter was able to reach our camp by driving his snowmobile over rocks, sand, and snow. He retrieved Wilson and left, and the police urged us to meet them. We had little choice, as to retrieve our massive load of haulbags would require several trips, and the prospect had become virtually impossible under the circumstances.

We carried camp to Sam Ford and the police took Dempster and Wilson to Clyde River. Four days had passed since the accident. Cowan, Shipman, and I waited for three more days for our outfitters, who told us that the unusually rainy spring had come early in the Arctic. We were the last remaining people in the region. A month had passed.

The Inuit gave us permission to name the mountain in Wilson's memory. I will remember Drew for his simplistic approach to life, sense of humor, amazing climbing skills, and his sharp intellect. I remember once, while discussing plans before the climb, I referred to it as a "project." Drew said, "I don't see this as a project. I'm just here in this beautiful place, under a beautiful wall, having fun climbing every day." I realized that the word did imply a sense of uneasiness and duty, but for Drew Wilson, life on the wall was the life he loved most. (Source: Peter Dronkers)

(Editor's Note: This is the first report of several on rappel failures in this year's report. See analysis of California's September 14 accident, page 40.)

FAILURE TO FOLLOW ROUTE—STRANDED
Alberta, Banff National Park, Mount Edith, South Ridge

On May 14, two male climbers (38 and 26) got lost while climbing the South Ridge of Mount Edith (2,554 meters) just west of Banff. They did not have very good information on the location of the descent route, although they had read about the route itself in a local alpine climbing guide. They began to rappel before reaching the summit, but ended up getting stranded above steep overhanging terrain on the Southwest Face. They were able to call for help on a cell phone. Warden Brad White said he initially spoke with one of the climbers by cell phone to try and nail down their location; however, where they were was nowhere near the descent route.

Analysis

People often research the route itself, but should also be doing some research on the descent route before heading out climbing. In this case they managed to find some features that kind of mapped their description of the descent. But by not having a real good understanding of where on the mountain the descent went and how difficult it was, they got themselves into trouble. (Source: Brad White, Public Safety Warden Banff National Park)

FALLING ROCK
Alberta, Mount Yamnuska, Belfry
On May 23, a climber fell 15 meters and broke both legs while attempting Belfry on Mount Yamnuska. He was with his climbing partner when a ledge broke beneath him and he fell. N.B. called for help and waited in the meadow below for rescuers to arrive. George Field, public safety specialist with Community Development, organized a helicopter sling rescue from the Canmore heliport. Although it was quite windy on the ground, conditions were better at a higher altitude near the accident site. "We were lucky we were in a bay and it was calmer in there," Field said. "We got as close as we dared to the mountain to get the patient out." The helicopter flew to an altitude of 6,600 feet, with a 100-foot rescue rope hanging underneath. Conservation officers flew up to the accident site to stabilize the injured climber. Then they put him into a screamer suit and hooked him up. One of the officers flew attached to the harness with the climber. The patient was flown to a staging area in the meadow below Yamnuska where he was put on an awaiting stretcher.
Analysis
Spontaneous rockfall and hold failure is common in this area because of the nature of the rock in combination with the winter melt and freeze conditions. This is evident in the large scree slopes below the cliff. For that reason, it is imperative that climbers be alert for rockfall and holds be tested before fully weighting them. (Source: Pam Doyle, Canmore Leader)

AVALANCHE, INEXPERIENCE
Alberta, Jasper National Park, Columbia Icefields, Mount Athabasca
On June 9, B.M. and N.Z. climbed Mount Athabasca via a variation of the standard North Glacier Route. They opted to descend the standard "ramp" route. The party triggered a class 2.5 avalanche. It swept them over some steep terrain features. They were not buried and came to a stop in the upper part of the debris. One sustained minor injuries while the other (21) had a broken ankle and compression fractures in his back. They called out for help. The avalanche that came down about 1:30 p.m. was about 300 meters wide and up to 80 centimeters thick in some places. The slide took them over some big seracs underneath them, and then they got carried down a few hundred meters onto the lower glacier.

A party walking on the glacier rushed to the aid of the young climbers, while a mountain guide raised the alarm, bringing in wardens from Banff and Jasper as well as an avalanche rescue dog. A party of three climbers helped them move down through the debris and away from the run-out zone. A heli-sling operation evacuated the climbers, equipment, and the wardens from the scene.

Analysis

A wet spring with large snowfalls and heavy rains in June and early July created poor travel conditions and extended an alpine avalanche hazard into the normal climbing season. A rain-soaked snowpack combined with various thin crusts and wind-loading created a winter type of slab condition on some slopes. Warm overnight temperatures allowed for only a mild freeze.

While the two climbers had some sport climbing experience, this was their first season of alpine climbing. They did not recognize the avalanche hazard, and the warmer temperatures in the afternoon contributed to the avalanche release. The climbers were also unaware of the alternative descent route through the AA Col, which is much safer. (Source: Garth Lemke, Public Safety Warden Jasper National Park of Canada, Cathy Ellis)

FALL ON ROCK, HAND-HOLD BROKE OFF
Alberta, Banff National Park, Lake Minnewanka Valley, Devils Gap, Macadamia

On July 31, a 30-year-old climber suffered serious injuries after falling 40 feet while leading Macadamia (5.9) near Devil's Gap in Banff National Park Sunday afternoon. The accident left the climber with a serious lower leg fracture and a crushed hand. Banff rescue wardens were flown to the scene. Alpine Helicopters flew him to Banff's Mineral Springs Hospital and later to a Calgary hospital.

Analysis

Spontaneous rockfall and hold failure is common in the Rockies because of the nature of the rock in combination with the winter melt and freeze conditions. Climbers should be alert for rockfall and holds should be tested before fully weighting them. (Source: Marc Ledwidge, Banff National Park Warden, and Cathy Ellis, *Rocky Mountain Outlook*)

FALL ON ICE
Alberta, Kananaskis Country, 2-Low 4-Zero

On December 3, I took a leader fall. The fall was a result of a left-hand tool plant shearing off a substantial block of very brittle ice while I was placing the other tool. The left tool proceeded to hit me in the mouth with some velocity, breaking a front incisor in half and causing a puncture wound on my lower lip. More importantly, the force of this hit caused me to lose my footholds, which were pretty good, resulting in a free-fall of four to five meters. The crampon on my right foot caught, severely spraining my ankle. I fell on a section that was largely vertical to overhanging below me, so I did not hit the ice with much force. I was leading on two ropes above a three-screw belay that I had set up maybe 40 meters off the ground. The force of the fall pulled my wife off her feet and against the anchors. (I weigh well over 200 pounds fully laden). I was suspended head down, pulled myself up, and placed a screw to clip off. I managed to climb up a few feet to retrieve an intermediate screw, then with some difficulty due to thin ice, set up an Abalakov with a "leaver" screw backup. Due to the sprained ankle I did not feel confident climbing back up to retrieve the screw, so I pulled the rope through, set up a double rope rap through the Abalakov, and rapped down. My wife rapped the same rig.

I did not feel the need for an evacuation. I was not critically injured, and although it is a substantial walk in to this climb, it is a largely easy trail. Additionally, we each had a ski pole, so with my wife carrying a heavier pack (bless her heart) and me using both poles, I was able to manage, albeit slowly. My feet were already somewhat cold due to the low temperatures, and I tightened the boot ankle on the injured foot, so it wasn't too painful.

I checked over and had the ankle X-rayed at the Canmore Hospital. The good news is that nothing was broken. The result was not being able to climb for several weeks due to damage to the ankle, and a broken tooth that could be fixed without a root canal. Very lucky, but a wake-up call.

Analysis

I was using Mammut Genesis 8.5 ropes. Probably the high degree of stretch on a single strand of skinny rope contributed to the lack of failure. There was little tension on the second strand. I had placed a stubby about three meters below the top screw, plus there was a screw about 1.5 meters above the belay. The belay was bomber—a stubby, an 18-cm, and a 22-cm R.C.L.

Lessons? Well, don't climb when it is close to minus 20 C. The ice can become particularly brittle. Additionally, this was a cold snap after a period of very warm temps, which probably contributed to chossy (sic) ice. Although I was on a climb that was well within my leading abilities and I wasn't having any particular difficulty, it was a bit hard to find good plants, and I was knocking off some big chunks. Under such conditions, additional care is obviously warranted. Plus, it just isn't very pleasant.

Although we had plenty of good clothing, if I had been more seriously injured and a rescue had been necessary, the clothing we had may have been insufficient to hold off hypothermia. We should have been carrying an additional insulating layer.

Ski poles are gold in the event of an injury. Walking out on my own accord would otherwise have been very difficult. This was my first (and hopefully last) leader fall on water ice. This is my eighth season water ice climbing. Although I have done quite a bit of soloing on easy water ice, this experience has cured me of that. I would have surely died without a rope. I was quite impressed with the holding power of the screw and belay chain, even in less than perfect ice. It also demonstrated the power of a good belayer and keeping cool heads. (Source: Edited from a report submitted to the website called Live-the-vision.com, name unknown)

FALL ON ICE
Alberta, Jasper National Park, Mount Kerkeslin, Kerkeslin Falls

On December 30, a party of two was climbing Kerkeslin Falls (III, 3), a moderate waterfall ice route in Jasper National Park. The leader was ascending the third and final pitch when he took a short fall. The ice screw that he had placed below him held. However, he fell onto lower angled ice below, resulting in a fracture of the lower leg. His belayer lowered him to a large ledge at the bottom of the pitch. Another party of three helped secure him and administered first aid. Two members of the second party descended the route and called for assistance. A warden service rescue team was dispatched and the injured climber and the other two remaining climbers were heli-slung off the climb just before dark.

Analysis

This accident illustrates how serious even a small fall on ice while wearing crampons can be. The injured party was lucky that a second group of experienced climbers were on the route and were able to descend quickly and call for help. If this were not the case, it seems likely that the injured party would have spent the night out before being rescued. (Source: Parks Canada Warden Service)

SLIP ON SNOW, EXCEEDING ABILITIES, INADEQUATE CLOTHING AND EQUIPMENT, NO HARD HAT, CLIMBING ALONE
British Columbia, Mount Robson Provincial Park, Base of Mount Robson

On May 23, M.S. and D.B. were camping at the Kinney Lake Campground. M.S. told D.B. he was going to "do some scrambling on the cliffs and gullies overlooking the campground" and would be back before dark. He never returned that evening. D.B. located the local rangers and reported him overdue. At first light, the rangers conducted a hasty search and found boot tracks about 800 meters above Kinney Lake in a snow gully. An RCMP helicopter subsequently located M.S. below a cliff in a gully. The Jasper Warden Service was dispatched and heli-slung the deceased climber out.

Analysis

M.S. was inexperienced in this terrain, had inappropriate footwear, lacked appropriate equipment (i.e. no ice ax for self arresting and no helmet), and was by himself. He likely slipped while on the snow slopes above the cliffs and subsequently slid and fell off a 30-plus-meter cliff. He likely did not survive this initial fall. He probably did not recognize the hazard of his position on the slope or consequences of a slip. (Source: Garth Lemke, Public Safety Warden Jasper National Park of Canada)

(Editor's Note: This individual was obviously not a climber. We include a few reports like this in hopes that neophytes will take heed.)

FALL ON ROCK, RAPPEL ERROR—PROTECTION PULLED OUT
British Columbia, Purcell Mountains, Eastpost Spire

On July 18, Dave Ireland (51) and Peter Uzieblo were about two pitches up Lions Way (5.6, six pitches) on Eastpost Spire. One dropped his digital camera, and so they were rappelling to retrieve it. Uzieblo did a mix of down-climbing and rappelling in order to lessen the weight on the rope. He then yelled up to Dave Ireland not to pull out on the anchor, only down. Unfortunately, the anchor failed Dave Ireland about a full rope length (60 meters) to the boulder field below, resulting in fatal injuries. In meeting with the Invermere, B.C., Coroner the day following this tragic accident, she advised that D.I. died instantly of a broken neck.

Peter Uzieblo is an accomplished and experienced climber. Dave Ireland was a novice with top-rope experience in Devil's Lake State Park (WI), but he could easily follow on 5.8 routes. He was a much respected and valued member of the Chicago Mountaineering Club. (Source: Edwina Podenski, Canadian ANAM editor and Paul Szymanski, friend of the deceased)

STRANDED—LEG STUCK IN CRACK
British Columbia, Purcell Mountains, Bugaboo Spire, Kain Route

On July 25, a male climber in his early 40s was climbing the Kain Route of the Bugaboo Spire (5.6) when his leg got stuck in a crack. Two Canadian Mountain Holiday (CMH) guides in the area initially climbed to the trapped man to make sure he was safe and secure. Banff rescuers Marc Ledwidge and Gord Irwin were slung to the scene by helicopter and were able to free the man after more than half an hour of tricky maneuvering. They brought kitchen oil from the CMH Lodge to lubricate the man's leg. "We put a rope raising system on him and tensioned him up, trying to figure out which way to move him to get his knee unstuck," said Ledwidge. "So with the combination of the tension system and just trying to move him back and forth a little bit, and the oil, we eventually got him free." (Source: Cathy Ellis, *Rocky Mountain Outlook*)

CORNICE FAILURE, AVALANCHE—DISREGARDED INFORMATION REGARDING SNOWPACK HISTORY, WEATHER
British Columbia, Mount Robson Provincial Park, Mount Robson, North Face

On July 28, a European mountain guide and a very experienced climber (38 and 49) left the Kinney Lake campground to ascend the Dog Buttress to a high bivy point for climbing the North Face of Mount Robson the following day. The route is described as a 50- to 55-degree slope overhung by large cornices and "three times as long" as Mount Athabasca's North Face, which looms above the Icefields Parkway.

When the men left their spouses, they said that they would return if they felt conditions were not safe. While there was no communication with the men after they left Berg Lake on July 28, that night the mountain was clear, making for a cool night and a tight snow pack. The next morning the women walked over to the ranger cabin in order to change campgrounds and extend their permits. From the cabin, they were able to see the climbers (through binoculars) making their ascent. On July 29, a local ranger observed them around the bergschrund at 6:00 a.m. On the other hand, the climber's spouses indicated that they last observed the climbers at 10:00 or 11:00 a.m. crossing the bergschrund. They seemed to be making fast progress up the route, climbing simultaneous and short roped, which indicated that conditions were good.

"Traditionally, you would want to cross the bergschrund a lot earlier than that," climber and helicopter pilot, Andre Lafferma, said. "In order for those guys to make the decision to start climbing the wall at 11:00 a.m., conditions must have been good," he said. After the two climbers disappeared into the clouds, Lafferma said that nobody really knows what happened. On July 30 at 6:00 a.m., the local park ranger, Chris Zimmerman, observed "two black lumps" at the base of the climb where none existed the day before. They were motionless and on avalanche debris at 10,000 feet below the North Face. Park Wardens from Jasper accessed the climbers via helicopter in poor light and visibility. Rescue wardens heli-slung into the site and verified both climbers were deceased from severe injuries and partially buried in fresh 2.5 avalanche and cornice debris. With the weather deteriorating rapidly, only one person was retrieved before the wardens were forced to exit the site. Wardens returned the following morning only to find that another size 2.5 avalanche had come down overnight. The remaining climber was not located. Several avalanches came down throughout the day further obscuring the site. The SAR effort was ended due to hazardous conditions.

Analysis

A wet spring with large snowfalls and heavy rains in June and early July created poor travel conditions and extended an alpine avalanche hazard into the normal climbing season. The area was now experiencing spring-like avalanche runs and warm overnight temperatures. The party climbed the North Face of Mount Athabasca the previous Monday after a rare overnight freeze, and conditions were excellent that day. They related these to what could be expected on Mount Robson but this was not the case. The weather had remained significantly warm in the Robson area.

They also checked several information sources, including the Robson info staff and the area ranger. All had recommended not proceeding due to hazardous conditions. The party did discuss this amongst the larger group but chose to proceed. They did not take out a safety registration with Robson Park. Garth Lemke said the pair was discovered largely because of "one of those bad-feeling-in-the-stomach kind of things" on the part of longtime ranger Chris Zimmerman, who had been watching the climbers through a spotting scope from across the valley. He had talked to these folks and got a bad feeling about their plans, had watched them in their progress, and then Saturday morning he looked up there and saw two black lumps at the bottom of the climb.

In his report to the coroner, Zimmerman said he observed the visible part of the route on a regular basis and did not notice anything out of the ordinary until the next morning. It was then that he noticed several car-sized cornice pieces amongst the avalanche debris. There was no witness to the accident; however, the climbers had severe injuries from falling a distance of potentially 2,000 feet if they fell from the summit ridge. (Source: Garth Lemke, Public Safety Warden Jasper National Park of Canada, and Andru McCracken, *Robson Valley Times*)

FALLING ROCK–PINNED CLIMBER
British Columbia, Purcell Mountains, Bugaboo Spire, Kain Route

On August 20, ten Golden Search and Rescue members responded along with Parks Canada and Canadian Mountain Helicopters to rescue a climber pinned under a rock on the Kain Route of Bugaboo Spire. The man (38) and his teenage son were descending when a large loose rock slid down and pinned him under a granite boulder that was about one and a half meters wide by three meters long and about 30 centimeters thick.

Emergency response personnel were called to the scene. They performed a heli-sling rescue after moving the rock with hydraulic jacks. The victim was pinned by the rock for approximately three hours before being flown to hospital in Cranbrook with a serious crushing injury to his left ankle.

Analysis

While the rock in the area is primarily granite, the routes do have some loose rock. Injuries or fatalities from falling or rolling rocks of various sizes are not uncommon. (Source: From a report by Kyle Marr, *Banff Crag & Canyon*)

FAULTY USE OF CRAMPONS–GLISSADING
British Columbia, Mount Robson Provincial Park, Mount Resplendent

On August 25, a party of four summited Mount Resplendent. On the descent, they chose to glissade a steep snow slope, near the base of the Mousetrap, below the Robson-Resplendent Col. They left their crampons on. They indicated that they had done exactly the same thing the previous day on the same route without incident. On this particular occasion, A.C. caught a crampon point on the way down and suffered what he believed was an ankle injury. He was able to limp down with some assistance from the party members and another party of three descending the same route. A.C. made the decision to continue the six-plus kilometers descent of the Robson Glacier on foot from the accident site to the base camp at Robson Pass. A.C. departed the camp the following day on a commercial helicopter flight.

He had sustained a broken fibula, going at 45-degree angle down to the joint. (Source: A.C., Jim Barrow)

Analysis

It is ill advised to glissade while wearing crampons. If the crampon points make contact with the snow surface during the glissade by mistake, the natural and obvious consequence is lower leg injuries.

FALL ON ICE
British Columbia, Mount Dennis, Guinness Gully

On December 2, a 35-year-old doctor from the Seattle, WA, area was descending from the route Guinness Gully on Mount Dennis near Field, B.C. when he tripped and fell 20 feet. They'd finished the climb and they were descending the same way by rappelling the ice climbing pitches. They'd rappelled the first pitch and were walking down some lower angle terrain to the next rappel when one in the party tripped and fell over about a 20-foot cliff. While one of the man's climbing partners stayed with him trying to keep him warm, a third climber rappelled to the road where he flagged down a tow truck driver, who called in the rescue.

Waning light made it impossible for the patient to be heli-slung from the site, forcing rescuers to climb the waterfall in the dark, hauling rope rescue gear with them up the frozen waterfall. The patient was immobilized on a vacuum mattress and lowered from the route in temperatures that dropped to –15 C.

He was taken to Banff Mineral Springs Hospital before being sent on to Foothills Hospital in Calgary. He suffered four fractures in his cervical and thoracic vertebrae, broken ribs, and a broken arm.

Analysis

It's not uncommon for accidents to happen on low-angle terrain when one's guard is down. Even a slight lapse of attention in steeper terrain can have consequences. We've all tripped at one time or another. (Source: Brad White, Public Service Warden Banff National Park, Dave Stephens, and Amanda Follett, *Banff Crag & Canyon*)

FALL ON ICE, INADEQUATE PROTECTION
British Columbia, Kootenay National Park, Haffner Creek

At about 11:00 a.m. on December 3, Banff Park wardens were called to a rescue at Haffner Creek, in Kootenay National Park, where a man in his 30s had fallen from an ice climb, according to public safety warden Lisa Paulson. The man was about 20 feet from the ground and about to clip his first ice screw when he fell, resulting in a broken ankle. He was rescued from the site by helicopter.

This isn't the first rescue performed at popular Haffner Creek, which is an easily accessed canyon off the Highway 93 South with a multitude of single pitch ice and mixed climbs. "With respect to that spot, a lot of people go there to practice," she said. "It's really well known. Everybody's really careful there but it's still been a few broken ankles pulled out of there."

While they were waiting to chopper out the patient, another climber took a four-meter fall and decked. Fortunately he managed to get up, dust off, and walk away. (Source: Edited from a report by Amanda Follett, *Banff Crag & Canyon*, and Joe McKay)

EXPOSURE, WEATHER
Yukon, Kluane National Park, Mount Logan, King Trench

An eight-member team from North Shore Rescue set out on May 7 to climb Mount Logan in the Yukon, Canada's highest peak at 5,959 meters (19,541 feet), to celebrate the 40th anniversary of the rescue organization. All were experienced mountain climbers who planned to take a month to complete their expedition. Climbing conditions are good in May because there are relatively few crevasses at that time of year. In the early part of their trip, the weather varied between storms and brilliant sunshine. One of the team members made it to the summit of Mount Logan. The others made it to secondary peaks, 40 meters (131 feet) lower, before deciding to turn around, partly because of the ferocious winds the climbers were battling. Alex Snigurowicz (45), Don Jardne (51), and Eric Bjornson (41) had started to head down on May 25 from the camp about 5,900 meters (19,400 feet) and were climbing across an exposed ridge when the weather started to change unexpectedly. "We could see it from a distance," said Snigurowicz. Quickly, the situation got exponentially worse, with driving snow and whiteout conditions. The three were trapped at 5,500 meters about 500 meters from the summit on Prospectors Col, which forms part of Logan's King Trench route. During their 48-hour ordeal, temperatures dropped to -30 C. "We were in the worst place you could be when it hit," Jardne said. "You couldn't see a thing. It was just coming at you from everywhere." They put up their tent and secured it with ice screws.

They spent the rest of that day and night being buffeted by wind, wondering if the tent would hold. Roaring blasts of wind pummeled the tent all night, at times so powerfully that the 175-pound Jardne, sitting by the tent's edge, was lifted right up. Frostbite was already setting into Bjornson's hands, causing enormous blisters, so Jardne and Snigurowicz decided, while the storm continued, that they should dig a snow cave in case something happened to the tent. Snigurowicz was in the entrance to the tent putting on his crampons and Jardne was already outside when the wind started lifting the tent with Bjornson still inside it. "I was trying to push it back," Jardne said, "but I just couldn't keep the tent down anymore." Without the weight of the two other men, the tent flipped, despite Bjornson's 240 pounds. His companions hauled him out and the wind sucked the tent away, along with a sleeping bag, shovels, their stove and a pack. Bjornson said the trio lost some of their gear when their tent blew away in the violent storm. "I could only grab so much stuff out of the tent before it went over the cliff. And one of the things I failed to grab was my overmitts, so I had my hands exposed for most of the time," he said, adding he was without the gloves for three days. "It was just one of those things you knew was going to get ugly," he said. "We had the tent tied in with ice screws and you could hear the fabric start to rip and once the tent was gone, I thought we were gone." With Bjornson wrapped in his sleeping bag and propped on skis and a foam pad in a rock niche, his partners spent six hours digging and scraping with a pot lid and ice ax to make the cave.

"When your life depends on it, you just work as hard as you can. We just huddled together in a snow cave and that helped keep ourselves warm and if you can't stay warm, you're gonna die," they said.

The three men huddled on two Therm-A-Rest sleeping pads with one sleeping bag between them. At dawn on May 27, the sun rose and the storm broke, allowing the trapped climbers to call for help on their radio to a fellow team member who had a satellite phone. The North Shore climbers were lucky. Through the combined actions of their fellow North Shore Rescue team members, the Canadian and U.S. parks services and U.S Air National Guard, they were rescued by helicopter from the mountain around midnight Friday and were flown to hospital in Anchorage. All three climbers suffered severe frostbite to their fingers and toes while they were trapped on the mountain.

Altogether, 24 personnel from the Kluane Park and Alaska took part in the operation, involving five helicopters, including a high-altitude Llama provided by the Denali National Park.

Analysis

Acting chief Warden Rhonda Markel credited the climbers' preparedness for saving their lives. "They were experienced climbers but there are risks and hazards out there," she said. "We all had radios between us so we could notify them of the problem and tell them what to do and that's what got the ball rolling," said Snigurowicz. On the afternoon of May 27, two others reached the trapped climbers and provided them with a tent until they were rescued on May 28. Park officials said those climbers were crucial to the success of the rescue. (Source: Various reports, including one from Denali National Park)

Canada's highest mountain measures in at 5,956 meters (19,541 feet), compared to 6,193 meters (20,320 feet) for Denali, the continent's highest peak. In the 22 years since the park was formed in 1973, there have been 18 deaths, of which 11 have occurred on Logan and seven in others areas of the St. Elias mountains. The climbing season for Mount Logan usually begins in late April and runs to late June, before the warmer temperatures have a chance to destabilize snow and ice conditions. Mount Logan is notorious for its sudden snow squalls that blow in from the Pacific Ocean. (Source: *Whitehorse Daily Star*, Chuck Tobin; Jane Seyd, *North Shore News*)

AVALANCHE, WEATHER, UNROPED
Yukon, Kluane National Park, Mount Logan, East Ridge
J.A. (22) and her partner C.D. (34) began their expedition on May 27. They were scheduled to return by June 25. J.A. had previously summited the King's Trench on Mount Logan at age 17, setting a record as the youngest person to scale the peak. She had also done the West Buttress on Denali. On May 31, J.A. was climbing at about 2,865 meters when a small avalanche swept her off her feet and down the East Ridge. The slide started about 20 feet in front of C.D., but missed him and hit J.A. instead. "It wasn't a big one, but just enough to kick her off her feet," said Rhonda Markel, Acting Chief Warden. J.A. fell 1,500 feet. The avalanche did not bury her, but it appears she died from head injuries. C.D. avoided the onslaught of snow and ice. He found his partner dead by the time he was able to reach her after descending from the 2,865-meter (9,400-foot) elevation.

The climbing team was not equipped with a satellite telephone. C.D. was unable to reach help for several days. Park officials only learned of the incident after J.A.'s partner waved down a Trans North helicopter.
Analysis
Markel indicated that it is likely that the rough weather climbers have experienced on the mountain so far this spring played a factor. She said there is an indication there was an abnormal buildup of wet snow on the ridge that came loose. Snow at that elevation would normally just blow off the ridge, but Markel suspects there was a buildup because of its heavy and moist condition. Markel said the thick layer of wet snow left by the storm likely caused or contributed to the avalanche. "I guess it was a pretty techni-

cal section. Why weren't they roped up? People are going to ask that. The reason is because of just what happened. They didn't want to pull each other off if something happened." (Source: No source cited)

(Editor's Note: In September, a solo climber on Mount Assiniboine did not return and no trace has been found as yet. Solo ascents on big mountains, especially in deteriorating weather, as was the case here, involve inherent risks.)

AVALANCHE, POOR POSITION, WEATHER, DECISION MAKING
Alaska, Mount Huntington

Trapper Creek climber Johnny Soderstrom (26) was declared missing and presumed dead in an avalanche, which occurred on Tuesday, February 15th. Soderstrom was last seen alive by his climbing partner, Joe Reichert, on Tuesday morning, as the pair approached the mountain's West Face Couloir route. After several hours of probing in avalanche debris in search of his partner, Reichert used a satellite phone to initiate search and rescue efforts.

Analysis

There is no way to soften the blow or somehow mitigate the ramifications of this tragic loss. Yet any lessons or benefits of learning from hindsight, I believe, must be seized. Johnny's death was felt far and wide by the climbing community, and many people can see themselves in this accident. It is only through the honest discussion of this incident that others might be safeguarded.

For the purposes of this report, the objective contributory causes will be discussed within the headings of terrain, weather, snowpack, and rescue. The subjective contributory causes will be discussed within the heading of decision-making/human factor.

Terrain. Based on statements made by the reporting party (Joe Reichert) and observations made during an aerial survey on February 16 and 17, the accident site appeared to have a slope angle from the high 30-degree range to the mid 20-degree range. Johnny appears to have entered the slide area at the steepest part of the slope.

Because it is at the base of the vertical West Face of Huntington, the slope lacks the typical windward (scouring) or leeward (loading) phenomena. Nevertheless, it is prone to snow slab formation, which results when snow sloughs from the adjacent cliffs and lands on the relatively flatter slopes below.

The slope is typical of a glacier in its lack of roughness or presence of sufficient anchoring. The slope is approximately 60 meters in height by 20 meters in width, is planar in shape, and lacks any compressive support from the snowpack below due to a large crevasse at the lower margin of the slab. The crevasse made the consequence of being caught in an avalanche a near-certain fatality.

Weather. There are two parts of weather to consider. The first is the prior events and how those may influence the stability of the snowpack. The second is how current events are influencing the stability of the snowpack. The question to be asked: "Is the weather contributing to instability?"

The unstable layering within the snowpack had its probable origins two weeks prior to the accident. A period of clear skies with no snowfall and cold temperatures from January 31 to February 5 resulted in a layer of weak, poorly bonded (faceted) snow on the top of the snowpack. This weak layer was subsequently buried by light snowfall on February 6 and 10, and further buried by an even heavier snowfall from February 13 through 15. February 11 and 12 were clear and cold, which continued to provide a sustained temperature gradient necessary to produce faceted snow.

The wind that Johnny and Joe experienced during the storm of February 13-15 (estimated 30+ mph) did not seem to contribute significantly to this avalanche. The slope is situated to avoid direct wind loading due to the lack of adjacent ridges or ribs, as evidenced by the relatively shallow crown face of the avalanche. However, the wind may have played a slight role at this location by acting as a compactor, making the slab more cohesive and able to propagate a fracture.

The weather on the day of the accident was stormy with heavy snowfall at times. This additional loading on this slope would have increased the avalanche hazard. Most avalanches happen during a storm, when the stresses on the snowpack are greatest and natural releases are most common. Consequently, it is prudent to avoid traveling in avalanche terrain during or immediately after storms.

Further, the overall visibility was less than adequate. The collection of information about the terrain becomes more difficult during storms or flat lighting. Communication is more difficult during bad weather, and good discussions—crucial to good decision making—are often minimized or non-existent. Finally, if there is an accident, increasing hazard on unreleased slopes or rebuilding hazard at the accident site may preclude optimum search efforts.

Snowpack. The snowpack, consisting of a layer of weak snow capped over by a slab, had stored elastic energy provided by the snow falling from the above cliffs. The weak layer and subsequent snowfall were ubiquitous, but the weak layer, slab, and poor bonding found at the accident site existed primarily at the base of the cliffs. It only needed the slight additional stress supplied by a suitable trigger—in this case Johnny—to put the snow in motion.

On the day of the accident, while traveling on the lower portion of the route, Joe noted a lack of typical clues indicating an unstable snowpack, such as other avalanche activity, collapsing layers, shooting cracks, or hollow-sounding snow. For a slab avalanche to occur, there needs to be a relatively strong layer over a relatively weak layer, a critical balance between the strength and the stress of the snowpack, and enough elastic energy to propagate a fracture. In this scenario, the weather events contributed to the strong-over-weak layering; the slope angle, while shallow enough to collect snow, had enough steepness to allow the snow to slide; and the cliff faces above provided the mechanism that built the slab and supplied the needed elastic energy.

Further, the stresses at this particular site would have been higher due to the lack of compressive strength that is typically provided by the adjoining lower snowpack. The snowpack on any given slope derives some support from running into the snow below that is on a slightly less steep slope. Because the bottom of the avalanche slope adjoined the open crevasse, it lacked this component. It is possible that this difference allowed Johnny to cross the similar slope to the left of the slide path without triggering it.

Rescue. From talking to Joe and examining the site, it appears that Joe did everything that could be done to locate Johnny. Because they did not carry avalanche beacons, Joe could only search for surface clues and search the debris using an avalanche probe. Johnny was most likely swept into the crevasse on the leading edge of the slab. Consequently, the probability of finding clues, because of the short distance Johnny traveled before entering the crevasse, was unlikely. Further, being on the leading edge would have made his burial very deep, so the chance of making probe contact was also low.

Joe first searched the debris that had not gone into the crevasse. This was a good strategy. The likelihood of a live recovery was highest there. He then concentrated his efforts in the main part of the debris in the crevasse, in the zone of highest probability of burial. Joe's probe method, while not standard, was the approximate spacing of the three holes per step and, using proper technique, could yield about an 80 percent probability of strike. This is within the range of acceptable probe-line probabilities.

Joe searched for an estimated two hours and twenty minutes. Considering the hazard of the continuing snowfall, potentially reloading of the slope, and the large overhanging cornices that he was required to search under inside the crevasse, this was an appropriate amount of time. Statistics compiled from thousands of avalanche accidents tell us that even during shallow burials, it is rare to find the victim alive after one hour.

Decision Making/Human Factor. In 95 percent of avalanche accidents, the victim or someone in the victim's party triggers the avalanche. In other words, the main cause of backcountry avalanche accidents is flawed decision making. Analyzing post-fatality decisions involves a certain amount of speculation. No one can know for certain the decision-making process that Johnny employed. Also, while retrospective judgments are easy to make, it is important to maintain a sense of humility. No one can predict with certainty how he or she might perform in a given situation, as many experts will attest. Even extensive experience and/or expertise do not provide absolute protection.

Based on the findings, it appears that the instability of the slope was underestimated, and the severity of the consequences was either not recognized or was underestimated. These judgments, particularly the latter, were the greatest contributory factors in this incident. Given the statement Johnny made immediately preceding the slide, it appears that he recognized the potential for an avalanche. However, he continued, either believing the snow would not avalanche, or that he would somehow be able to survive a slide.

Neither Johnny nor Joe dug a pit to investigate the layering and bonding of the snowpack. This is understandable given that a pit site that could provide the necessary information regarding slab formation, stress concentration, and layer bonding was exposed to the very hazard they were attempting to avoid. Sometimes in mountaineering "digging a pit" increases one's exposure-time to the hazard. For this situation, however, the clues could have been garnered from a recollection of the weather, an examination of the snowpack lower on the route, knowledge of the slope angles they were likely to encounter, and an understanding of how slabs are built at the bottom of cliffs.

Joe and Johnny had spent longer on the route than anticipated, and the shorter amount of time they had remaining may have affected their decision to push forward on that day rather than wait for better conditions. They did, however, have a plan of calling for a flight to pick them up if time got short, though this was not their preferred option.

The entire mitigation of the avalanche hazard had to be the avoidance of avalanche slopes. This was not accomplished. Micro route selection was poor. On the macro scale, the route left little room for variation. The nature and location of the crevasses pushed the route up under the cliffs and above the crevasses. The route up to the point of the open crevasse was acceptable, but once Johnny stepped above the crevasse, the situation changed completely. To avoid being placed between a hammer and an anvil, as it were, it was necessary to skirt along the sides and upper edge of the slab. The margins of the slab are identifiable by the serac on the left side, the bergschrund above, and the lower slope angles on the right side.

The visibility was variable, so it may have been that Johnny couldn't see the alternative option of ascending toward the bergschrund before he crossed above the open crevasse. Also, the alternative route could have necessitated taking off ones skis and post-holing, or at least making numerous switchbacks and side-stepping, all of which would be difficult in deep snow. Other factors may have influenced Johnny's decision making. The distance from where he entered the avalanche slope to the safer lower angled slopes ahead is short. He was concerned about avalanches, which was demonstrated by his instructions to Joe. A predictable level of apprehension would have made the lower-angled terrain on the other side of the slope a very enticing focal point, a situation not conducive to looking around for alternatives.

It was unfortunate that visual contact was not maintained. This was an understandable product of the type of terrain they were attempting. From an avalanche perspective it is acceptable and often beneficial to travel unroped and farther apart. Being separated may have prevented both of them from being caught. It's unknown how deep Johnny was pushed into the crevasse, but with the amount of snow involved, it is highly unlikely, had they been roped together, that Joe would have been able to arrest the fall and not be pulled in himself.

The decision to not take avalanche beacons deserves discussion. A beacon would probably not have made a difference in the outcome of this tragedy. However, a beacon would have provided more information about where exactly Johnny was buried and helped to eliminate the inevitable uncertainty and discomfort that occurs when a body cannot be found. Beacons also enable rescuers, including organized responders, to focus their efforts, shortening the search time and limiting their exposure to potential hazards.

Using an avalanche beacon in the big mountains has benefits other than body recovery. There are potentially survivable avalanches even in the big mountains and having a beacon does increase the odds of survival. The Mount St. Elias avalanche of June 10, 1981, provides a clear example of the potential benefits of wearing transceivers. Survivor of a burial Charlie Campbell said, "On my eight previous climbing expeditions, none of us ever used avalanche beacons. It was at my insistence that everyone had to wear one this trip. I guess I got smart just in time. Our choice of route, the intentional separation of our party, our avalanche beacons, and the fact we were trained to use them all helped stack the deck in our favor."

The absence of beacons often represents an overestimation of one's ability, or an underestimation of the hazard. It is not uncommon for experienced mountaineers to feel that if conditions make it prudent to wear a beacon, then the conditions are too dangerous to proceed. These climbers often claim that they "just won't go" if it's unsafe. Indeed, if wearing of a beacon encourages or allows the user to travel in more dangerous conditions than they might otherwise travel in, then there is a loss of overall safety. But to say that dangerous avalanche conditions will be totally avoided is a serious overestimation of any person's ability to recognize and deal with the hazard. To say it another way, it is a serious underestimation of any person's ability to make mistakes and not see the entire picture, or subconsciously to eschew the data that contradicts a desired result. Judging the hazard of any given slope is like shooting at a moving target. Conditions change over time, and what may be totally safe to cross on one day may not be safe on the next.

There are many factors that allow individuals to recognize the potentially serious consequences of avalanches and yet think that their personal situation is not so dangerous. In fact, studies on cognition have shown that people consistently rate their hazard evaluation skills significantly above average. We all feel we're smarter than average and consequently feel the hazard is not as great for ourselves as it is for others. (Source: Blaine Smith, Alaska Avalanche School/Alaska Mountain Safety Center)

FALL ON SNOW, INADEQUATE CLOTHING AND EQUIPMENT, INADEQUATE PROTECTION, FATIGUE
Alaska, Mount McKinley, West Buttress

In 2004, the Humphrey twin brothers Jerry and Terry (55) along with Jerry's son Jeremy, climbed on the West Buttress in late May. Departing on May 24th, Jerry and Jeremy reached the summit on June 4th (11 days), while Terry, who was experiencing the effects of an upper respiratory infection, stayed behind at their 17,200-foot high camp.

The trio returned this year for another climb of the mountain with one of the goals being to have Terry go to the summit. Jeremy signed up as a solo climber with plans to attempt one-day ascents from the 14,200- foot camp. The three departed on April 29th, traveling together up to the 14,200-foot camp where the twins continued on to the 17,200-foot camp on May 8th. This was nearly a month earlier than the previous year's climb. Most years, climbers find colder conditions and more exposed ice. This year was no exception.

On May 7th, Jeremy made a one-day ascent of the upper West Rib and descended via the West Buttress. Below Denali Pass he encountered a short six- to eight-foot section of vertical ice that had formed since last year's season. Jeremy stated that this small step was the most difficult section of climbing he had encountered that day. He expressed these concerns to his father and uncle upon returning to the 14,200-foot camp. As quoted from his trip chronology, he stated, "Very dangerous up there, nothing like in 2004." On May 9th, the brothers took a rest day at the 17,200-foot high camp in preparation for their summit push the next day. On the 10th, both the Humphrey brothers and Jeremy departed from their respective camps for a summit attempt.

The following is Jeremy's account: "I leave camp at 8 a.m. in bitter cold. I climb to the top of the Messner at the Football Field in 4 hours exactly making it 12 noon. I try to call T and J, but get no answer. Two hours later I am on the summit sharing it with two Swiss climbers (Suzanne and Fran). I rest there in cold but sunny weather for about 45 minutes. I am tired and have a headache, but relieved to be heading down. The six-hour dash to the summit has taken more out of me than I thought it would. I try to call T and J again with no answer. I pass many climbers on the way down, but still no T and J.

"Finally, I encounter Terry and Jerry near the Japanese Weather Station. I estimate the time at roughly 4 to 4:30 pm. I am not happy to see them so low on the route so late in the day. Jerry looks anxious about how far they have to go, and Terry looks exhausted. They are not roped together. I do not mention it. They are using one ax in self-arrest grip and one ski pole in the other hand, a reasonable combo that I use myself.

"Jerry asks me, 'Do you think we can make it?' I ask, 'Why are you moving so slowly?' Jerry rolls his eyes at me. Terry leans over, out of breath. I tell Jerry, 'Yes you can make it, but you are moving so slowly you should go down.' A stupid oxymoron of a sentence brought on by my fatigue and belief that Jerry would bring them through. I point out some clouds that have surrounded the summit. They are not threatening but just obscuring the visibility up there. They would later dissipate becoming a non-factor as seen in the summit pictures.

"Jerry changes the subject, not letting my advice deter them. He is worried about me because I look beat up. My face is sun burnt and swollen from the cold and altitude. They try to give me food and water, but I refuse insisting that they need it more than I do. I am cold standing still in the wind, so I prepare to move on. I wish them luck. I tell them to keep their radio on and be careful. I ask about the route around the Denali Pass bergschrunds. Jerry tells me the first is steep, then turn left and out flank the second one by going almost over to the rocks."

The following account is provided by Clark Fyans, a guide for Mountain Trip: "On the morning of the 10th, the brothers left for the summit between 11:00 a.m. and 12:30 p.m. There were approximately 15 climbers ahead of them attempting the summit. One of the climbing groups was a guided Mountain Trip group of 6, led by Clark Fyans. As Clark ascended the traverse from camp to Denali Pass, he fixed pickets to protect his team during the ascent and descent. A total of 10-11 pickets were placed and used in conjunction with NPS pickets placed in previous years. One picket was also placed on the summit headwall.

"Clark's group reached the summit at 4:15 p.m. and spent about an hour on the top. On the descent from the summit headwall, he encountered a three-person rope team from Zurich heading towards the summit. Clark offered to leave all of his protection in place for them to use on their descent for safety and they agreed. When the Mountain Trip team approached the football field (19,500 feet), they came across Jerry and Terry. Terry continued to move slowly toward the summit as Jerry chatted with the group for about five minutes. He was very casual and spoke of his plans to climb Everest in 2006. Clark expressed a concern for their slow pace late into the day, and Jerry stated that Terry was moving slowly and was really tired, but they had planned to descend late in the night. Clark explained that he was leaving the protection in for the other climbing team and they would be welcomed to use it. Jerry said it would be of no use to them because they had no ropes or harnesses, only ice axes and crampons. The Mountain Trip group continued to descend and arrived at camp at approximately 7:00 p.m. When the three Zurich climbers returned to camp at about 10:00 p.m., they expressed concern to Clark about the brothers. They said that they were moving very slow and that Terry looked extremely tired. They were last seen as the Zurich climbers descended the summit headwall at about 8:00 p.m. Jerry and Terry repeated to the Zurich climbers that they were expecting to have a long day and to descend late. Knowing that the brothers had a FRS radio to communicate with Jeremy at Camp 3, Clark put his radio on scan for the entire evening in the event that they called for help."

The three Zurich climbers (Altitude High 2005) led by Andrei Lenkei were the last to see the brothers alive. As they were descending from the summit ridge at 2000, they met Jerry and Terry half way up the final slope to the ridge. Lenkei reported that Jerry looked real strong while Terry was really struggling to make any upward progress. During this brief encounter, Terry was observed stepping around a small crevasse. Jerry was near him continually encouraging Terry with every step. They noticed that Jerry had a pack while Terry only wore his jacket. The Zurich party had concern for their welfare and Lenkei's personal opinion of this situation was that they should turn back and go down. They asked the brothers about leaving in the pickets on the traverse below Denali Pass and Jerry responded, "Don't leave the pickets in, take them out. We don't have a harness or rope."

It took the Zurich team about four hours to descend and they went to sleep around 1:00 a.m. on June 11. Lenkei reported that he looked up toward the pass at this time and the brothers had not yet come into view.

The following statement is the discussion Jeremy had with his father by radio an hour our two before the accident: "At a time that I can't confirm or even speculate on, I am awakened by Jerry on the radio. He asks am I OK. I say yes and ask, 'Where are you?' I have to ask about 5 times before the radio is clear enough for him to understand. He answers, 'At the Japanese Weather Station.' I ask, 'Are you guys OK?' He says yes, but the transmission is breaking up, so he will call me in one hour at the bottom of Denali Pass. I am worried about him, but an intense fatigue forces me to sleep. I did not receive another call."

Clark Fyan's account continues: "The next morning Clark checked their snow cave to see if they had returned at 8:30 a.m., and when he found it empty, he called the Rangers at the 14,200-foot camp below on the FRS radio to see if they had made any contact with them. Jeremy, who was also monitoring the radio, stated that he last heard from them at about 10:30 or 11:00 p.m. the previous night. They were at the Japanese weather station just above Denali Pass.

"At 9:00 a.m., Clark spotted two objects approximately 1200 feet below the Denali Pass traverse in the Upper Peter's Basin. NPS Climbing Ranger Karen Hilton agreed to have Clark first-respond to the objects. Due to the lack of radio coverage between Camp 3 and the Peter's Basin, a member of the Mountain Trip team, Guy Cotter, would remain at camp and act as a radio relay. Clark Evans and Mark Sedon, also a member of the Mountain Trip team, roped up and carried sleeping bags, two liters hot water, food, and first-aid equipment. About 15 minutes from High Camp, they encountered the two subjects about one meter apart. Jerry was face down and Terry was on his left side, both heads orientated the same direction. No heartbeats were present in either of them. Terry had obvious trauma to his left forehead and his left shoulder. His outer insulated jacket was zipped open, and had on only liner gloves. Jerry also had obvious head trauma. His insulated pants were ripped and around his knees and he had bare hands. They had no ice axes.

"Denali Pass was hard, wind-packed snow with little or no blue ice. There were two large bergschrunds blocking the traditional route. One was located just as elevation is started to be gained, and the other was about two-thirds the way up the traverse. The lower bergschrund had a small bridge that made it easily passable while the upper bergschrund had a two-meter vertical section of very hard snow. One picket was placed just below the vertical section, and another about 5 meters above.

"The bodies were found [on the] fall line of the vertical section of the upper bergschrund. It is assumed that one brother was probably attempting to help the other down-climb the vertical section."

At 9:45 a.m., Ranger Karen Hilton notified the Talkeetna Ranger Station of the Humphrey's overdue status. At 11:05, Fyan notified Hilton that the two were confirmed deceased. The weather was flyable so the NPS contract Lama Helicopter was put on standby for a possible recovery of the bodies.

At 2:23 p.m. the Humphrey's were extracted from the 17,200-foot camp and short-hauled directly to the 7,200-foot basecamp and then flown to Talkeetna.

Analysis

The following observations were made of Terry and Jerry's last camp in a snow cave at the 17,200-foot camp by Ranger Joe Reichert on June 12th: "The final camp occupied by the brothers was a small snow cave at the 17,200-foot level on the West Buttress. The cave was approximately 50 feet west of the NPS rescue cache. Clark had looked in it on the morning of

June 11 to determine that the party had not returned. When I moved the shovel and snow blocking the entrance, the first items encountered were a rope, two harnesses and the associated climbing safety protection. Under and behind this equipment were their sleeping bags, food, and cooking equipment. All of the gear was dusted with snow that blew in through the entrance that was not completely sealed. It appeared to me that they had initially planned to use the safety equipment and made a last minute decision to leave it behind."

Analysis by Daryl Miller: "The Descent of Denali Pass has been the primary catalyst for climbing accidents on Mount McKinley. There have been more than 100 reported accidents resulting in eight fatalities since 1960. The snowy and sometimes icy trail that traverses up a 30- to 40-degree slope from the 17,200-foot high camp to the 18,200-foot Pass is very deceptive. Climbers are typically hydrated and at their strongest when ascending the pass at the beginning of their long summit day. The opposite is true on the descent at the end of the day, with some climbers physically and mentally exhausted as well hypoxic and dehydrated.

"At the time the Humphrey Brothers would have been down-climbing, the light would have been extremely flat and near dark on their descent from Denali Pass, with sub-zero temperatures. Because their fall was not witnessed, the exact manner and just how it happened can only be speculated. One theory that would appear to be supported by the fall line in the snow is that the brothers were attempting to down-climb the two-meter steep section and one fell into the other, causing both to fall approximately 1,000 feet.

"It is unclear why the brothers chose not to take their rope and why they didn't turn around and descend when moving so slowly. It is my professional judgment that these men were more than likely exhausted and had no chance of self-arrest when they fell. In my 24 years of climbing on Denali, my most perilous moment was in 1991 descending Denali Pass after a rescue with another mountaineering ranger. We were both exhausted and hypoxic from managing a lowering of a stricken climber at 19,800 feet. Our descent took almost two hours of roped and careful down-climbing, belaying each other as we descended. I can only imagine how difficult it must have been for Terry and Jerry who had no way to protect them from a slip or fall. This tragic accident served as a harsh reminder early in this climbing season that Denali Pass is still a very dangerous and an unforgiving section of the climb."

HACE AND HAPE
Alaska, Mount McKinley, West Buttress
On June 8, the "AAI-1-Taylor" expedition arrived at base camp to start their ascent of the West Buttress. The team arrived at the 14,200-foot camp on

the evening of June 14, which is very close to the recommended rate of ascent of 1,000 feet per day.

After the first night here, Taylor reported that Michael St. Denis (46) exhibited signs of fatigue and malaise. On May 16, St. Denis spent most of the day in his tent. Around 1730, Taylor noticed that St. Denis was becoming confused and less aware of his surroundings. Recognizing the deteriorating condition of his client, he decided to take St. Denis to the Ranger Camp for an assessment. St. Denis was diagnosed as suffering from both high altitude cerebral edema and high altitude pulmonary edema.

NPS Ranger Gordy Kito, in consultation with NPS volunteer physicians Dr. Jim Freeman and Dr. Jim Sprott, determined that due to the patient's persistent ataxia, they would not attempt to walk St. Denis down the mountain, as it could take multiple days and that falling because of a loss of balance was inevitable.

St. Denis was evacuated from the 14,200-foot camp to Talkeetna at 1200 on June 18 via the Lama helicopter and then transported to Alaska Regional Hospital in Anchorage.

Analysis

The ability of the guide, Dylan Taylor, to recognize that his client was exhibiting the signs and symptoms of HACE and his quick actions to get him to the Ranger facilities where oxygen was available contributed to the favorable outcome of this incident. Although it is less likely for a climber to be afflicted with HAPE or HACE if they climb at the suggested rate of 1,000 feet per day, it is by no means a guarantee that a person will not suffer from altitude illness. The recommendation of 1,000 feet per day is only a guideline. Everyone will react differently to altitude, even those who have been to altitude previously. Each time someone goes to altitude there is a possibility that he or she will suffer from AMS, HAPE, and/or HACE regardless of past performance at altitude.

It is of some note that those who suffer from HACE may have persistent neurological manifestations that can last for days, weeks, and even months. The fact that these symptoms may persist for extended periods of time must be considered when determining whether or not individuals should be allowed to descend under their own power, with assistance from their team, and when it is appropriate to evacuate them by other means. (Source: Daryl Miller, South District Ranger)

DEHYDRATION–FROSTBITE
Alaska, Mount McKinley, West Rib

At 1600 on May 27, both members of a Spanish expedition "Dos Perdigones en la Cassin" began their ascent of the Upper West Rib. As the team approached the summit around 0500 the following morning, they recorded winds of 30 mph and a temperature of -40F. Adraino Martin (31) took off his glove-shells and, wearing only mid-weight liners, took photographs for several minutes. Martin was first aware of a cold injury to his fingers as they rested along the football field at 19,000 feet. The two descended the West Buttress and arrived at the 17,200-foot camp at 0930.

Martin's partner contacted NPS Ranger staff and VIP Sprott reported Martin as having "significant" frostbite on both hands. Climbers John Varco and Sue Nott volunteered to assist Martin down to the 14,200-foot camp. All four climbers descended without incident, Martin being short-roped. NPS ranger Shain and VIP Falley met the descending climbers at 15,200, but no assistance was needed.

Examination by the Ranger staff at the 14,200-foot camp revealed numbness and marked discoloration down to the first and second phalanges on all fingers except the thumbs. Patient history revealed that Martin and his partner had collectively consumed less than three liters of water since the start of their climb and had not slept in 32 hours. Given the extent of Martin's injuries and the weakened state of the two climbers, a continued descent to the 7,200-foot camp was deemed unsafe. NPS staff decided to re-warm Martin's injury, realizing that blistering would further inhibit a safe descent.

NPS staff continued care of Martin's injury until weather allowed for an air evacuation. At 0930 on May 30, Martin was evacuated by NPS Lama helicopter to the 7,200-foot base camp and transferred to a fixed-wing aircraft off the mountain for further treatment.

Analysis

Being dehydrated was most likely the largest contributing factor to the extent of Martin's injury. The team stated that neither of them had taken any water at the onset their summit attempt and that of the four liters they brought with them, one froze. Taking off his over-mitts for several minutes on the summit undoubtedly compounded the situation. Climbers attempting the summit by any route are encouraged not only to bring extra water and a thermos, but a stove and fuel so they can maintain their water intake in the event of a mishap. (Source: Daryl Miller, South District Ranger)

HAPE, ASCENDED TOO FAST, FAILURE TO FOLLOW INSTRUCTIONS
Alaska, Mount McKinley, Cassin Ridge

On the evening of June 14 the "Princes of the Puff of Smoke" expedition arrived at base camp to start their ascent of the Cassin Ridge. When the team arrived at the 14,200-foot camp on the evening of June 17, Bryan Feinstein (22) complained of feeling weak and short of breath. His companion, Barry Hashimoto, told him to rest in their tent while he made a carry to the West

Rib Cut-off (15,800 feet). When Hashimoto arrived back at camp, he found Feinstein weaker and vomiting. The following morning, after advice from an Alaska Mountain School guide, Hashimoto contacted the Rangers and brought Feinstein over to the NPS camp.

Feinstein was diagnosed as suffering from advanced high altitude pulmonary edema. Feinstein was evacuated from the 14,200-foot camp to Talkeetna on June 20. Talkeetna Ambulance EMT's examined him. At this point Feinstein refused further treatment and, against NPS recommendations, did not attend a physician or hospital for further assessment.

Analysis

As with all people climbing on Denali and Foraker, this team received a thorough briefing at Talkeetna Ranger Station from a Ranger with 30 years of climbing experience in the Alaska Range; however, they disregarded the advice about acclimatization and the way to approach a serious Alaskan climb. The suggested rate for acclimatizing is based on substantial medical research. It was totally ignored by Feinstein and his partner. It is surprising, in fact, that Hashimoto did not also appear to suffer from the effects of altitude.

The team's lack of understanding about the seriousness of Feinstein's condition led to exacerbate the condition. When the first signs and symptoms appeared, they could and should have descended and dealt with the situation themselves, following good mountaineering practice. As it was they delayed until Feinstein's condition deteriorated to a point where he was incapable of descending under his own power or even with assistance. There is little doubt that he would have died if the NPS Rangers had not been there to provide aggressive medical treatment.

Another troubling aspect of this situation was the apparent desire of Hashimoto to pass on this problem to the NPS so he could get on with his climb, regardless of the fact that he was jointly responsible for the potential death of his teammate. Perhaps this persistent desire to summit was driven by the fact that they were grant recipients, in which case Hashimoto may have felt he had a greater responsibility to their donors than to his teammate.

Climbers need to realize that the NPS is there to assist, but that does not mean one can abrogate tacit responsibilities toward teammates. (Source: Edited from a report by Daryl Miller, South District Ranger)

AMS AND FRACTURE
Alaska, Mount McKinley, West Buttress

In June, lead guide Bill Allen of the guiding concession Mountain Trip brought client Joanne Devenish (42) to the 14,200-foot medical camp because she was turned around short of the summit, about 19,700 feet. The guides subsequently brought her down to the 14,200-foot camp for medical evaluation. After this patient was treated, lead guide Vern Tejas of Alpine Ascents International asked the Ranger staff to examine client Rosemary Zimmerman (49) who had sustained a lower leg injury while descending the fixed lines. Both were treated and flown off the mountain three days later.

Analysis

The Mountain Trip client started having respiratory difficulty while on a summit bid. Her guides, against her protests, turned her around and descended to the 17,200-foot high camp and started a Diamox regime of treatment. Her condition did not improve so the entire expedition descended to the 14,200-foot medical camp.

This climbing group had adhered to a reasonable ascent schedule. The patient had not exhibited any signs of AMS previously. Devenish stated that she had experienced approximately two hours of blurred vision near the summit, but that it had cleared up upon descent. She was unable to maintain oxygen saturation and had to be placed on high-flow oxygen to assist with respirations. For this reason, it was determined that the patient would be unable to safely descend the mountain under her own power. She was evacuated via the Lama helicopter on June 26, along with Zimmerman, who was also unable to walk down.

Injuries and illnesses are to be expected during a mountaineering expedition and, unfortunately, can occur regardless of planning. What is significant with these two cases is that both clients were evacuated/assisted down to the 14,200-foot medical camp without NPS assistance. In the case of the Mountain Trip expedition, the guides recognized a potentially fatal medical condition occurring and, against their client's desires, brought her down safely to a place where she could receive medical care.

Both groups demonstrated self-sufficiency and good judgment. In addition, in both cases guides remained with their clients until their conditions were resolved. (Source: Daryl Miller, South District Ranger)

RAPPEL ERROR—ANCHOR FAILURE
Arizona, Sycamore Canyon, Paradise Forks

On November 5, Shelley Windsor (31) had been climbing on several routes at Paradise Forks, Sycamore Canyon with her climbing partner Mark Brenner (26). During the climbs and rappels, the anchors had been constructed on large, live pine trees with one-inch nylon tubular webbing slings, connecting the end loops of the slings with a carabiner that was then attached to the rope.

Prior to the accident Mark led a climb and then belayed Shelley up the same climb. Upon reaching the top of the climb, she disconnected, then pulled the rappel rope and retrieved the anchor slings from the rappel anchor tree. She then took the rope and the anchor material to a different tree in preparation for a rappel to end up where their backpacks were. She constructed a new anchor around a large, live Ponderosa pine tree (approximately six feet six inches in circumference and approximately 31 feet from the cliff edge) and was preparing to rappel as Mark walked toward her after packing his gear from the previous climb.

When Shelley began to weight the rappel, Mark saw the anchor come apart. The slings were no longer attached to the tree. Shelley fell approximately 90 feet to the canyon floor.

Other climbers in the area were notified of the accident and one of them made a call for help. Bystanders did an assessment and began first aid while waiting for rescue. Due to the relative remoteness of the area (approximately 20 miles from the nearest EMS units and approximately 40 miles from Flagstaff), rescue units had a significant response time to the scene.

After being extracted from the canyon, Shelley Windsor was transferred to an air ambulance and flown to Flagstaff Medical Center where she was pronounced dead.

Analysis

Ms. Windsor was wearing a commercially sewn seat harness and a helmet at the time of the accident. She used an ATC-type rappel device, according to Mr. Brenner. The climbing rope appeared to be in good condition and the webbing found at the bottom of the cliff was in good condition and was still tied into a sling. The auto-locking carabiner appeared to be in good condition other than some minor damage from the fall.

The two slings (described by Mr. Brenner as ten-foot runners when tied —but possibly longer) used for the anchor were the same color. This could have caused difficulty in inspecting the set-up.

It appears that Ms. Windsor may have intended to girth hitch two slings together and subsequently wrap the linked runners around the tree, but somehow an error was made in the connection, and when weighted, the slings came apart. One possibility is that the girth hitch was tied around a bight of the second sling and not through the sling. In this configuration, it may appear that the slings were connected correctly and would bear some weight if tested without full body weight prior to the rappel. Once full body weight was applied to the system, it could fail. Another possibility is a knot-jam, which could have been caused by the knot of one runner being pinned against the tree trunk by the bight of the other runner under tension. This configuration might initially bear some weight but could also fail after repeated loading and unloading associated with the edge transition during rappel.

To reduce the likelihood of a similar incident from occurring, a suggestion is to use a more easily inspected anchor system when wrapping trees, possibly incorporating different colored slings if connecting them together is foreseen. It's always a good idea to have one's partner inspect the system. (Source: Aaron Dick, SAR Coordinator, Coconino Country Sheriff's Office, Jed Williamson, and local climbers)

FALL ON ROCK—HANDHOLD CAME OFF, FAILURE TO TEST HOLD
Arizona, Camelback Mountain

On December 26 K.P. (female - 46), L.R. (male - 53), and T.N. (female - 50ish) went out to climb on Camelback Mountain, a park area located centrally in Phoenix. L.R. is a very experienced lead climber and K.P. and T.N. had been lead climbing for about a year. K.P. and T.N. completed leads on The Monk, starting on the 5.7 variation for the East Face route. It was a beautiful day and they were having lots of fun. The group of three then went about 100 yards over to the Camel's Head to do Hard Times on Gargoyle Wall, a bolted 5.7. After K.P. and L.R. each led the first pitch, T.N. took her turn on lead. About 45 feet up, T.N. decided to move laterally, maybe five feet, to move onto easier looking terrain where T.N. saw a juggy nice hold. She was right below the next bolt on the route. She had both hands on the hold and began to pull herself up without testing the hold. The hold broke. Unfortunately, she was ten feet from the last bolt, so between the pendulum and the rope stretch, she fell about 25 feet, struck the rock, and broke both legs at the ankles.

There was enough rope to lower her to the ground, where cell phone contact was made with emergency rescue personnel. Another out-of-state climber who is a paramedic was nearby and helped stabilize both ankles. T.N. did a crab walk/crawl about 200 yards to the top of the Headwall where a rappel was made to an area accessible to hikers. At the bottom of the cliff members of the Tactical Rescue Squad of the Phoenix Fire Department placed T.N. on a stretcher and hand-carried her to the parking lot about half a mile from the accident site.

Analysis

For interested climbers: Camelback Mountain consists of a mudflow breccias and fluvial sediments described as "petrified mud" in Opland's guidebook *Phoenix Rock II*. The nature of the rock and the scouring summer sun can take their toll on rock quality. (Source: Erik Filsinger, Secretary, Arizona Mountain Club)

FALL ON SNOW—LOSS OF CONTROL ON VOLUNTARY GLISSADE
California, Mount Whitney

On April 10, Patrick Wang (27) and Martin Kozaczek (27) climbed the Mountaineer's Route on Mount Whitney. On descent, around 14,000 feet, there is a steep traverse on a snowfield between the summit and the notch. The climbers decided to remove their crampons and attempt to glissade. Kozaczek went first and began to slide too fast. He was able to self-arrest.

Wang began his descent and immediately began to slide too fast. He attempted unsuccessfully to self-arrest. He tumbled out of sight over a rock band. His body was found the next day.

Analysis

Wang was reported to be an experienced mountaineer. Snow conditions were consolidated, windblown, and icy. The traverse is short in distance, but is the most technical portion of the climb. Due to the short distance, the consequences of a fall are often overlooked.

Many choose to climb/descend un-roped and unprotected here. There have been numerous fatalities at this same location. In fact, there was another fatality here within one month of this one involving a solo climber who was wearing crampons but not carrying an ice ax. There was another accident in the same place in October resulting in serious injury. (Source: Gregory Moss, Sequoia District Ranger and Chris Waldschmidt, SAR Coordinator for Sequoia/Kings Canyon National Parks)

FALL ON SNOW—LOSS OF CONTROL ON VOLUNTARY GLISSADE, IMPROPER CLOTHING
California, Mount Baldy

On April 16, veteran California mountaineer and author Robert (R.J.) Secor (48), glissaded out of control 1,200 vertical feet from near the summit of Mount Baldy to level snow near the Sierra Club's Baldy Hut, where rescue volunteers stabilized the seriously injured climber. A helicopter evacuation occurred four hours after the fall.

An eyewitness said: "He had his ice ax and his yellow overalls on. He was seated and began to glissade. He lost control very quickly and failed to self-arrest. He tried very hard to. Then he hit the rocks and tumbled down all the way. He started down from the same spot as I did just behind me. It was a terrible accident to watch."

Another reported that it was likely his ax was lost in the fall and that his crampons were ripped from beneath his pack where he keeps them, because they were not with his things or in his car.

He sustained fractures of the shoulder blade, ribs, and skull.

Analysis

Mount Baldy is a familiar and convenient destination for a lot of us here in Southern California that has the same objective dangers as other alpine peaks have: it's easy for us to think of it as a benign "local mountain" and to forego precautions we would take on more serious mountains.

One climber said, "I saw him putting on the yellow slickers and thought 'Well, he's going for a fast one!' He lost control very quickly…" (Source: Robert Speik, from an interview with SAR personnel, and *Backpacker*)

VARIOUS FALLS ON SNOW
California, Mount Shasta

There were seven climbing-related accidents on Mount Shasta last season, with most of them being on the Avalanche Gulch route. With a smooth snow surface, we had a few climbers who fell and tumbled 1,000 or more feet, suffering only bruising and large abrasions. Injuries from other incidents included, tib/fib fracture, fractured ribs, torn knee ligament, and abrasions.

The accident of note last year was June 12, when a man (age unknown) fell over 1,000 feet on the east side. Apparently, he had descended from the summit through a steep section of the Hotlum-Wintun route and was putting on his skis, and standing on a 40-degree slope when he fell. Another climber hiked out and notified Siskiyou County Sheriff Search and Rescue of life-threatening injuries to the fallen climber around 12,000 feet on the Wintun glacier.

We had windy conditions that day, and earlier on the south side of the mountain, a climber had literally been blown over by the wind and fell 1,000 feet—but suffered only minor injuries. Because of the wind, four USFS Climbing Rangers and two SAR volunteers could be flown only to around 8,500 feet. When the rescue party arrived at the scene, the injured climber was conscious and stable. He had injuries to head, shoulder, lower back, hip, and knee.

A lowering system had to be constructed. Fortunately, at last light, winds decreased and he was short hauled by CDF Helicopter 202 to an LZ at 8,500 feet, where he was transferred to a CHP helicopter with a paramedic on board and flown to Mercy Medical Center. He remained in the hospital for several days. He was released with several lacerations on his head, bone chipping on the skull, a broken jaw, dislocated shoulder, large hematoma to the lower back, and torn ligaments in his right knee.

Climbing Mount Shasta in perfect conditions has a certain amount of risk. High winds increase that risk, and in my opinion, this was not a good day to climb. Crawling to the summit in high winds is NOT courageous or noble. Turning around and descending to safer elevations is. (Source: Eric White, Climbing Ranger/Avalanche Specialist, USFS)

STRANDED, WEATHER, INADEQUATE CLOTHING, FOOD, AND EQUIPMENT
California, Yosemite Valley, Higher Cathedral Rock

On May 15, Christopher Simmons (26) and Emily Craft (28) became benighted on the eleventh pitch of the North East Buttress route on Higher

Cathedral Rock. They were rescued by park personnel, who went to the summit and lowered fifty feet to the climbers, providing them with dry clothing and then hauled them to the summit. They walked down.

Analysis

Simmons is 5.12. sport and 5.10 trad leader. Emily leads 5.11 sport, but had done no trad leads. This was their first long route. It has lots of chimneys but they had never climbed chimneys before this. They had left headlamps behind, had insufficient clothes, only one rope, and made a late start. The top pitch is confusing and they got lost at dark. They tried to find a way out and finally called for help by cell phone. (Source: John Dill, NPS Ranger, Yosemite National Park)

STRANDED, WEATHER, DARKNESS, INADEQUATE CLOTHING, INEXPERIENCE

California, Yosemite Valley, Royal Arches

On June 16, Deana Barone (25) and Yoshiko Miyazaki (27) started up Royal Arches (5.7 AO, 15 pitches). Though neither had done the route before, they planned to complete it well before dark and then descend by the North Dome Gully.

Route finding proved harder than expected, as did some of the climbing. They completed the last pitch just before dark. As it got dark, the team could not find their way through the last section. Spring run-off made the climbing more difficult than usual and various off route "use trails" led them astray. To make matters worse, a storm front moved in and it began raining just after dark. Stuck just below the valley rim without warmth and rain or bivy gear, they decided to call for help.

Rescuers reached them late that night and escorted them safely down North Dome Gully. (Source: Lincoln Else, NPS Ranger, Yosemite National Park)

Analysis

We had agreed from the beginning that Yoshiko would lead every pitch and that we were not going to take a second rope to rappel, but instead descend the North Dome Gully in the dark, even though neither one of us had done it before. We had only climbed (together) one other time. One party passed us at the bottom of the first pitch and another around the sixth pitch. Storm clouds rolled in, loud winds obstructed our communication and route finding became an issue. We were traversing slowly across wet, slippery, exposed slabs. We lost sunlight at the top of the last pitch and could not figure out how to get ourselves off the final ledge.

Never again will I climb with someone whom I had only been climbing with once before on a long route. I will always bring a second rope so I can rappel if needed. I will never let more than one party pass me along the way. *Always* will I be prepared for a High Sierra storm. This experience has taught me that there should always be two leaders—never one leader and one follower. It has encouraged me to learn how to lead climbs and start getting my act together. (Source: Deana Barone)

Royal Arches has been climbed round trip in under an hour, but epics and rescues are common on this "easy" route. Why? Like many other "moderate" trad climbs, the route is frequently underestimated. While the technical climbing is relatively straight forward, the climb as a whole is far more challenging than its rating might indicate. The route finding is difficult, the level of commitment is high, and for many teams the descent is a larger challenge than the route itself. (Source: Lincoln Else, NPS Ranger)

FALL ON ROCK
California, Yosemite Valley, Lembert Dome

On July 5, John Hrizo (36) was injured in a lead fall of about thirty feet on the second pitch of Northwest Books on Lembert Dome (5.6, 3 pitches).

According to Hrizo, he did all the leading, followed by his partner, Stacy Waksmonski (29). After they climbed the first pitch, Hrizo climbed to an intermediate belay midway through the second pitch where he rigged a belay. Because Waksmonski was a relatively inexperienced climber, Hrizo wanted to break the pitch into smaller pieces for her.

After belaying Waksmonski up, Hrizo began to lead the second half of the pitch. He had with him a copy of the *Supertopo Guide to Tuolumne Meadows*, and from it he concluded that the right-curving crack above and to the left of the belay was 5.9, harder climbing than he intended to do. Hrizo placed a #3.5 Camalot just above the belay and began to climb the face to the right of the crack.

Initially, the face climbing was easy, around 5.6. But as he climbed higher, he began to suspect that he was off route. Ten feet above the Camalot, he decided he was definitely off route and that the crack to the left was where he wanted to be. He stopped and assessed his options.

Hrizo thought about down-climbing, but didn't want to down-climb on slab. "The slab seemed to keep the same angle, then flatten out some and meet the crack," said Hrizo. He decided to press on to the crack. Although the slab didn't get steeper as he continued up, "it got pebbly" in texture, with small loose rocks that made foot placements uncertain.

About fifteen feet above the Camalot, Hrizo began concentrating on foot placements, but his climbing shoes kept picking up pebbles that made his feet slip. "I cleaned off my shoe and replaced it several times," he said, but could not get a secure foothold. He started to down-climb and traverse left to meet the crack when his feet suddenly slipped.

Because of the angle of the slab, Hrizo slid down the wall instead of free-falling. His hands and forearms were badly cut and gouged in the process. Part way through the fall, Hrizo's feet hit a small ledge. "I hit the ledge, jammed my ankles, and kept going," he said. He was flung out with enough force to badly bruise his leg when he pendulumed back into the wall. Waksmonski's belay stopped him after he had fallen about thirty feet.

Hrizo said he knew right away that one ankle was broken and the other was probably sprained. His arms and hands were bleeding. Waksmonski belayed him as he climbed fifteen feet back up to the belay station, where he tied in and pulled the rope. Together they splinted the obviously broken ankle with the Supertopo Guide and tape. Hrizo then re-rigged the belay into a rappel and, with an autoblock back-up, rappelled to a lower ledge with his knees against the wall. Once Waksmonski joined him, Hrizo repeated the process three more times (they had only one 60 meter rope) until they were on the ground.

Ranger Fred Koegler received a vague report of a fallen climber with injured ankles on Lembert Dome. From the Lembert parking lot, Ranger Koegler hiked to the northwest side of the dome to search for the patient. Koegler found Hrizo near the base of the route. Hrizo calmly reported what had happened while Koegler assessed his injuries and began initial treatment. The Tuolumne SAR Team and several of Hrizo's friends carried him in a litter about a quarter mile to the parking lot. He declined further care from NPS and his friends drove him to Mammoth Hospital, where he was diagnosed with two badly broken ankles.

Analysis

Hrizo showed uncommon grit, focus, and pain tolerance in getting himself and his partner safely off the wall. His initiative turned what would have been a high-angle rope rescue into a simple litter carryout, drastically reducing the danger for his rescuers.

More importantly, Hrizo self-rescued without compromising his safety; he carefully rigged his rappel anchors and remembered to use a backup on his rappel (the autoblock: very important with slippery, bloody hands.) Self-rescue is great, but for your sake and for the sake of your rescuers, don't compromise your safety to do it. Better to be plucked off the wall with minimal injuries than rushed from the base with critical ones.

Being comfortable down-climbing will help you recognize and use the right time to retreat when you're in this dilemma. You can practice down-climbing each time you top-out a route on top-rope; instead of being lowered to the ground, down-climb the route. First, though, be sure your belayer can belay you safely down the route.

Not all belays are equal. Waksmonski's belay was effective because she was attentive to and had good communication with Hrizo, and because the belay was rigged so that the force of the fall was taken by the anchor, not by the belayer. Otherwise, Hrizo's injuries could have been worse and Waksmonski could have been injured from the force of the fall as well. (Source: Lincoln Else, NPS Ranger, Yosemite national Park)

FALL ON ROCK—HANDHOLD CAME OFF, CLIMBING ALONE, LEFT NO INFORMATION ON WHEREABOUTS
California, Yosemite National Park, Tuolumne Peak

On July 15, at 4:30 p.m. I (Jeff Moore, 27) was injured when I dislodged a large rock while climbing a short Class 3-4 chimney on Tuolumne Peak in Yosemite National Park. I was climbing alone collecting data for a research project on exploring rockfall. I had not informed anyone of my itinerary, carried no cell phone, and was not wearing a helmet.

The research project had taken me to nearly the same spot the previous Monday to determine rates of cliff erosion by rockfall. On this Friday I had completed 2 sites and was heading for a third at a large cirque amphitheatre on the southeast flank of Tuolumne Peak near Tuolumne Meadows.

Approaching the site, I was stemming an inside corner when I grabbed a hold above my head and dislodged a large rock. The rock was about twice the size of my chest and it came free from the wall easily, causing me to fall about 15 feet in an upright position. While falling, the rock was at the level of my chest and I fought to move it away from my body. During the fall, the rock crushed my left ring finger, nearly severing it, and struck my right forearm, opening an eight-inch gash and destroying much of my forearm muscle. I landed on my feet and badly sprained one ankle. (At the time I thought it was broken.)

I assessed my situation, noticing significant bleeding from my right forearm. Both bones in my arm were visible but neither was broken. My right hand was rendered useless due to the muscle injury – clasped closed without the opposing muscles required to keep it open. I quickly dropped my backpack and took off my shirt to wrap my arm, at which point I was alerted to my left finger injury. The finger was almost totally severed, dangling by a small thread of tendon, but was not spurting blood. At the time, I considered pulling it off to ease my descent but did not. The combined injuries left me without dexterity, making it difficult to wrap my shirt tightly around my open arm wound.

Looking up, I could see Tenaya Lake four miles in the distance where my car was parked and where I would find help. I cursed myself for not having a cell phone but was thankful I was able to walk. Before descending, I opted to re-shoulder my backpack which had in it a treated nylon jacket, long underwear top, water, food, headlamp, maps and aerial photos, a compass, and an emergency space blanket, none of which I could easily retrieve due to my hand injuries. I placed my left hand atop my right forearm so the shirt would soak up the blood from both injuries and did my best to hold both arms above my heart.

I began descending over steep slabs, ledges, and boulders within one or two minutes of my fall. I had studied maps of the area well and knew there was a trail some 2,000 vertical feet below the accident site, but in attempting to follow the most direct route, I was stopped by terrain too steep to descend in my condition. Backtracking and moving to a lower-angle route, I reached the trail in about one hour, during which time I suffered the first of two very painful tripping incidents. I remembered from the maps that once I reached the trail I should head in a counter-intuitive direction, away from Tenaya Lake, before the trail would swing around to the proper heading. Unfortunately, I arrived at the trail in a different place than I thought I would, and after walking for about a half an hour, I realized I was heading the wrong way. I turned around and hiked out.

During my two hours hiking on the trail I was badly attacked by mosquitoes: I was covered in blood, wearing no shirt, and couldn't fend them off with my hands. This stands out in my mind as being the worst part of my day. I also fell another time while crossing a slick-rock stream, which, aside from being painful, soaked my cotton pants. I encountered no other people on the trail.

I reached the highway at 7:30 p.m., three hours after the accident, and immediately flagged down a car. It slowed, looked me over, and drove on. Another car came by shortly and drove me to the Tuolumne Meadows ranger station.

Analysis
• Testing holds. Although I had been testing holds that day, I did not test this particular one, maybe because of its large size. I should have been more aware of loose rock, especially since I was climbing alone.

• I was not wearing a helmet. The terrain leading up to the section where I fell was never harder than Class 2, and in preparing for the trip I didn't envision needing a helmet. However, I was out studying rockfall, so wearing a helmet was probably appropriate. I should not have climbed the chimney without a helmet.

• Nobody knew where I was or when I planned to return. Due to circumstances (family and friends out of town), I had not told anyone of my itinerary for the day. There are a number of people I could have easily informed and did not do so.

• Hiking and climbing alone. Climbing alone warrants particular vigilance for the considerations listed above. Specifically, informing others of your itinerary and using extra caution are critical, and I failed at both.

• I feel that a cell phone would have helped me get assistance sooner, even though reception is limited in the mountains. Carrying one could mean the difference between life and death, and I now feel it's worth it to always bring one along. (Source: Jeff Moore)

FALL ON ROCK, INADEQUATE PROTECTION, MISUSE OF EQUIPMENT (GRIGRI), NO HARD HAT
California, Yosemite Valley, Half Dome

On September 14, a clear day, Bela Christopher (Chris) Fehrer (35) was solo climbing the slab route when he fell 100 to 150 feet to his death.

Analysis

With dozens of Yosemite routes under his belt, including Mescalito, Wyoming Sheep Ranch, El Capitan (seven times), and a host of other hard walls, he was by no means a beginner. He was likely headed up the slabs to shuttle gear to the base of Tis-sa-ack (VI 5.9 A3+) in preparation for a solo climb.

Known to climbers as the "death slabs," this approach, though much shorter than the nine-mile maintained trail around the south face, is notorious for loose rock and devious exposed fourth-class route finding. According to friends, he knew the approach well from previous Half Dome ascents. On this day he didn't follow the "standard" approach, a goat trail of sorts that zigzags across the slabs taking advantage of broken ledge systems. Instead, he headed up a more direct, steep corner system avoided by other climbers. After a short pitch of fourth class, he left most of his rack on a ledge, rigged a quick single-piece anchor, and rope soloed with a Grigri up a moderate fifth-class pitch. He placed a few nuts and cams as he went and built a three-piece anchor upon reaching the end of his rope.

Exactly what happened next will remain a mystery, but the climber fell before successfully clipping into his anchor. Rock fall has always been common below Half Dome's northwest face, and this climber's top anchor was surrounded by exfoliating flakes held in place by dirt and sheer luck. Though other causes are possible, a moss scar found while investigating the accident suggests he was standing on one of these flakes when it cut loose. As he fell, he ripped two of the four pieces he placed on the pitch. He tumbled down the slabs and landed on a large ledge just as his rope came taut on another piece. Two climbers found his body attached to the lead line by a Grigri, apparently having fallen the length of the pitch.

Beyond the objective loose-rock danger, rigging mistakes may have played a roll as well. When the climber was found, his Grigri was set on the lead line in the direction appropriate for a single-rope rappel from the top anchor, not in the direction one might use while rope soloing up from the lower anchor. As a result, his Grigri never truly came tight on the line; the rope wrapped around his body as he tumbled, ripping two pieces when it came tight, but his Grigri never engaged. In the end he stopped only by hitting a large ledge.

It's possible that he rigged his Grigri backwards before rope soloing the pitch and then slipped on loose rock before clipping to his top anchor. In this scenario, his Grigri would have slid down whatever rope remained before wrapping on his body as he fell. Since his protection failed, the orientation of the Grigri ended up being irrelevant, but it suggests another scenario. He may have re-rigged his Grigri for a rappel at the top of the pitch, intending to anchor his lead rope and rap back to his lower anchor, but somehow failed to connect his lead line before leaning back to rappel. There was a figure eight tied in the end of the rope, possibly intended as his anchor point, and his Grigri was attached to the line just a few feet from this knot. Whatever its intended role, in the end this knot never held any weight. In any case, there are some lessons to take away:

1. When you place protection, make it count. Whatever the cause of his fall, this climber placed very little gear on the pitch, and two of these pieces failed. The others (including his single-piece lower anchor) were sketchy at best. He was a skilled trad climber, and confidence on easy terrain could explain these careless placements. If he had taken the time to find solid protection despite the moderate grade, he might have survived his unexpected fall, assuming he had also rigged his self-belay properly.

2. Back to basics: double-check your rigging. Much of the rigging in this accident appeared to have been rushed or carelessly done. If the climber had clipped into one of his top anchor pieces before dealing with the rest of his anchor, his fall would have been caught immediately. Had he rigged his Grigri correctly, it might have arrested his fall sooner. If he was attempting to rappel, a quick double-check of his anchor attachment could have saved his life. Remember the basics; these safeguards are what prevent absentminded mistakes.

3. Know where you're headed and take loose rock seriously. Though it's possible he was intentionally taking a variation to the standard slabs approach, it's more likely that he was off route. With better information to guide his decision-making he might have turned around before heading into seldom-traveled terrain. Climbing popular routes spoils some of us into a sense of security, but it only takes a split second to realize that dirty, loose, easy fifth-class can be more dangerous than clean, sparsely protected 5.10.

4. Use the right device. Though many soloists use it, the Petzl Grigri is not intended as a self-belay device. Its manufacturer strongly warns against using it for this purpose—it's very easy to rig a Grigri backwards, rendering it useless for catching a solo fall. The standard sliding clove hitch or one of a number of belay devices designed for self-belays are more foolproof.

5. Wear a helmet. This climber wasn't wearing a helmet despite the approach's ominous reputation, and head trauma likely played a role in his death. Though a helmet can't protect us against everything, it might have prevented this tragedy. (Source: Lincoln Else, NPS Ranger, Yosemite National Park)

FALL ON ROCK—RAPPEL ERROR, NO HARD HAT
Colorado, Eldorado Canyon State Park, Rincon

On January 26, a 25-year-old man was fatally injured when he fell 20 to 30 feet in Eldorado Canyon State Park. The Boulder County Sheriff's office said the accident occurred at about 6:15 p.m. as the victim was rappelling. He was not wearing a helmet and sustained severe injuries when he landed on his head. His climbing partner summoned emergency help, but the victim was pronounced dead as he was being evacuated from the canyon. (Source: Edited from articles appearing in *Rocky Mountain News* and *Boulder Daily Camera*)

Analysis

Rincon is a crag in Eldorado Canyon with generally mid to upper range difficulty climbs 5.9-5.12 up to three pitches. Rincon is also a climb that is rated 5.11a. One normally does not rappel off it. (Source: Leo Paik)

FALL ON ROCK, INADEQUATE EQUIPMENT—SANDALS, OFF ROUTE, NO HARD HAT
Colorado, Boulder Canyon, Near Security Risk Crag

On April 2, a 31-year-old male was attempting to set up a top-rope system when he suffered a fatal fall from a rock outcropping near Security Risk Crag.

Analysis

The victim was attempting to set up a top-rope for his climbing party, consisting of himself, his sister, and his girlfriend. The victim, wearing only sandals, free soloed a traverse toward a location where he thought there were anchor bolts. He reportedly slipped three times as he traversed before finally falling. His head impacted on the rock three times during the fall. He was not wearing a helmet.

The party reported that they thought they were at Security Risk Crag, located well above the roadway in Boulder Canyon, when in fact they were on an unnamed outcropping much closer to the road. (Source: Rocky Mountain Rescue Group)

FALL ON ROCK, INADEQUATE BELAY—ROPE RAN OUT
Colorado, Boulder Canyon, Animation

On May 24, Eric Gurvin (19) sustained injuries to his back, ankles, and wrist when he fell 20 to 30 feet when the person lowering him ran out of rope and dropped him.

He had finished climbing a 5.9 route in Boulder Canyon known as Animation and was being lowered to the ground from a top rope about 4:00 p.m. There was another climber with them.

Analysis

As he was being lowered, Gurvin's belayer was unaware that the end of the rope was approaching and allowed it to slip through the belay device used to slow the descent.

This cliff has a number of routes longer than 30 meters per pitch. Thus, it sets up folks who climb with 60-meter ropes to need a second rope. Many sport climbers these days do not bring a second rope. (Source: Edited from an article in the *Boulder Daily Camera*, with added comment by Leo Paik)

FALL ON SNOW, WEATHER, GEOLOGY
Colorado, Maroon Bells, Bell Cord Couloir

On May 30, Kip Ryan White (49), an experienced climber and indie singer-songwriter, died in a fall in the saddle between North and South Maroon Peaks outside Aspen. White and his son Jordan (19) fell 400 feet while descending the 50-degree, narrow, east-facing Bell Cord Couloir. The climbers were belaying one another, unanchored, when one of them lost purchase. Jordan, knocked unconscious, with his helmet split open on a rock, awoke moments after the accident to find his father 40 feet downhill and already dead.

Suffering from a mild head injury himself, Jordan down-climbed 600 feet of steep terrain before beginning a two-mile descent to Maroon Lake. He spent a cold, exposed night under a patch of trees before hiking out early Tuesday morning to drive his father's truck to the Aspen Valley Hospital.

Analysis

The Bells have a grim history. "There used to be several fatalities a year," Lou Dawson, a prolific climber and guru of Colorado fourteeners, told the *Aspen Daily News*. "A rope is problematic if the rock is loose because there's no place to anchor it." The notoriously loose Bells have claimed other local mountaineers, including Greg Mace, a prominent member of Aspen Mountain Rescue. The relative danger of the Bells, coupled with their easy access, have led the U.S. Forest Service and Mountain Rescue Aspen to call them the "Deadly Bells" as a warning.

Mountain Rescue Aspen believes that the weekend's poor weather contributed to unfavorable snow conditions—a thin crust layer over several inches of mush—causing the father-and-son team great difficulty in self-arresting once their fall began. "You just keep sliding," Dawson told the newspaper. "That's what happened to Greg Mace, and he knew what he was doing."

Kip White had summited numerous fourteeners since moving to Colorado in 1979. The father-and-son team had endeavored to be cautious on South Maroon Peak, and turned back at the 13,800-foot saddle because of deteriorating weather. (Source: Edited from a report by Courtney Belcher, news@bigstonepub.com)

FALL ON ROCK—INADEQUATE PROTECTION, OFF ROUTE, INEXPERIENCE
Colorado, Boulder Canyon, Eagle Rock
On June 5, J.H. (20) and Z.T. (20) were climbing the Great Dihedral, a 3-pitch, 5.5 trad route in the infrequently climbed Eagle Rock area of Boulder Canyon.

J.H. began leading the second pitch, which the website describes as: "Climb slabby rock with little pro as it steepens... you will see a fixed pin under a large roof, don't go that high but traverse left on scary moderate ledge to a slab that brings you up and left and into the dihedral (scary moves above tricky pro)…"

He fell 60 feet before Z.T. caught him on belay. J.H. impacted the rock face and sustained a compound tib/fib fracture, a maxillary nose fracture, and multiple cuts and bruises.

Analysis
J.H. did not traverse left as described and had difficulty finding gear placements. He unknowingly climbed off route to clip a series of three fixed pins under the large roof. He used very short quickdraws rather than long runners, which created a high degree of rope drag as he traversed left into the dihedral. Here again, J.H. had difficulty finding gear placements. He spent several minutes trying to place a micro-nut, but ultimately gave up. The slabby face above seemed relatively easy and J.H. could make out a ledge where he assumed the bolt anchor would be. He decided to "run it out" on this section and 10 to 15 feet below the ledge he slipped.

The climbers lacked adequate information on the difficulty of the climb, in terms of both rating and gear placement. First, novice leaders should ensure that they select climbs well within their limits. Multiple sources of information would have been very helpful in this case. Second, climbers transitioning from sport to trad may often be accustomed to following a bolt line, and therefore face route-finding challenges. Third, recognizing when and where long runners should be used can also be problematic for sport climbers. In this case, the use of quickdraws created severe rope drag which made the "easy" slab section that much harder. Fourth, running it out always increases the distance of any fall. Finally, the ledge where J.H. assumed the two-bolt anchor would be was in fact 10 to 20 feet below the actual anchor.

It should be noted that the fact that he was not wearing a helmet did not contribute to the severity of his head injuries. (Source: From a report by the Rocky Mountain Rescue Group)

STRANDED—RAPPEL ANCHOR FAILURE
Colorado, Capitol Peak

In June, Kevin Smith (32) was rappelling with a partner on Capitol Peak, a 14,000 foot peak with a Grade IV 5.9 North Face route and a classic "knife-edged" hiking route about 14 miles west of Aspen, when his anchor gave way and left him stranded as a result of his climbing rope falling with the anchor. He was about 80 feet off the ground.

Smith's climbing partner, Doug Shepherd (23), was not able to reach with a rope and left for help at about 1:30 a.m. Shepherd had to hike about eight miles in the dark. The sheriff's office did not receive information on Smith's whereabouts until 8:55 a.m.

A rescue team from Mountain Rescue Aspen got a climbing rope to Smith about 3:30 p.m. Sunday. He rappelled down and hiked out on his own. (Source: Edited from the *Rocky Mountain News*, June 20, 2005)

FALL ON ROCK, INADEQUATE PROTECTION, ROCK BROKE OFF, NO HARD HAT
Colorado, Garden of the Gods, Three Graces

In mid-August, a young male local climber died as a result of a fall from this formation. In talking with the search and rescue folks, I learned that he was climbing up the south ridge on the easternmost of the three slabs of rock that make up the Three Graces. He climbed up about 30 feet without protection, put in a cam behind a four-inch thick flake, and fell on the first move above the flake. A 12 x 12-inch chunk of the flake broke off as the cam expanded. The climber fell straight down about ten feet, then apparently his feet caught on the rock and he flipped over and landed headfirst.

Analysis

Climbing this ridge may be relatively easy, but good protection is virtually nonexistent. In addition, the rock is rather funky, even by Garden of the Gods standards, and is even worse given the rains of the past couple of months. Climbing too high to a first protection point, counting on a cam behind a flake of weak, possibly wet sandstone, and not wearing a helmet may have all contributed to this tragic accident. (Source: From a posting by Bob Hostetler on www.climbingboulder.com)

FALL ON ROCK
Colorado, Black Canyon of the Gunnison, Escape Artist

A 37-year-old climber fell yesterday afternoon (October 23) at the Black Canyon of the Gunnison National Park while ascending the Escape Artist route on the North Rim wall. Nearby climbers witnessed the fall and were able to reach the climber who fell approximately 60 feet. The unidentified climber's protection held him on the wall until other climbers were able to lower him to the base of the climb. National Park rangers were notified at 5:00 p.m. and a rescue team was assembled. A Montrose County Fire Department paramedic reached the patient at approximately 10 p.m. The climber suffered possible pelvic and femur fractures and is in stable condition. He was evacuated to the Montrose Community Hospital. (Source: Edited from the NPS Morning Report)

FALL INTO BUILDING—MISCALCULATED PENDULUM SWING FROM CRANE
Colorado, Boulder

On December 6, Ryan Young and Jacob Fuerst climbed over the chain-link fence surrounding a University of Colorado construction site, and walked straight to the base of the towering yellow crane. It was about 3:00 a.m., 28 degrees F, with enough ambient light from a nearby classroom building to see. Wearing warm clothes and backpacks, the 22-year-old friends scaled the middle of the crane's square tubular tower, pulling themselves up hand-over-hand, accustomed to the effort, and not talking much.

"We knew what we needed to do," Fuerst said. They climbed up and around the crane operator's box and arrived at the boom—a triangular steel tube they estimated to be longer than the 125-foot crane was tall. They worked their way out to the boom's tip end, which extended across 18th Street and over an alley between two buildings below.

They thought the boom had been left angled in the perfect position for the giant swing off of it they were about to attempt. They calculated that they would swing through the alley and whoosh within five feet of the ground, before soaring back up above the buildings.

"We liked to go get where people had not gone before," Fuerst would say later. "It seems like these days, that's hard to come by. It's especially even harder in Colorado to get up in faraway places and do what no one's ever done."

Even though they hadn't taken a jump this daring before, they craved the adrenaline rush that would follow. They unzipped their backpacks and extracted two 200-foot climbing ropes, some webbing, and carabiners. They secured two pieces of webbing to the crane tip, as anchors, and attached their climbing ropes to the anchor with carabiners. They then retreated about 90 feet along the boom, back toward the center of the crane, until their ropes pulled almost taut against their hip and chest harnesses.

Young would go first. He extended his arms wing-like, preparing to take flight. And then he hopped off the 12-story crane into the night. Fuerst watched as the rope took control of Young's plunge. He would say later that he couldn't see anything going wrong until it happened.

Young's swing carried him with lethal impact into the side of the CU power plant building, a trajectory much like that of a wrecking ball. Passersby said they heard a loud crash.

"He went right into it," Fuerst said. "Then he didn't move." (Source: From an article by Chris Barge, *Rocky Mountain News*, December 10, 2005)

Analysis

This incident was not included in the statistical data. It was chosen to illustrate how variations on extreme sports need to be thought through. Ryan Young, from all reports, was an enthusiastic, fit climber, who had also taken up sports such as skydiving. A closer profile can be found at the following website: bargec@RockyMountainNews.com (Source: Jed Williamson)

(Editor's Note: Our new correspondent who took responsibility for Colorado narratives this year lost all her work as a result of a computer problem. Therefore, only these few reports appear. There were at least two other fatalities and several serious falls – including a rappel failure at the Ouray Ice Festival, but the editor did not have enough details to print instructive reports.

No data or reports from Rocky Mountain National Park were submitted this year.)

FALL ON ROCK, MISCOMMUNICATION—INADEQUATE BELAY, CLIMBERS UNKNOWN TO EACH OTHER
Maine, Bald Mountain, Shag Crag, Tightrope

Jed Piatt (29) of Dover, N.H., was in a group of experienced climbers when he fell from the route Tightrope (12d) on Bald Mountain's Shag Crag shortly before 6:00 p.m. Steve Allarie, District Game Warden for the Woodstock area, said Piatt fell 15 to 25 feet. He suffered broken ribs, a broken ankle, and a slight concussion.

"Based on his injuries, he had to be hand-carried down the mountain in a basket," Allarie said. "It was very difficult because of the steep terrain and it was nighttime."

The LifeFlight rescue helicopter was able to land near Reading Road in Woodstock, and took Piatt to Central Maine Medical Center in Lewiston, where he was treated and released Sunday.

Analysis

Always go over your verbal signals, especially if you and your partner don't know each other. Piatt called, "Take," and the belayer thought he wanted rope to clip so let out slack instead. Also, be wary when using a 9.4 mm rope in a Grigri. Due to the extra slack and force generated from that, the 9.4mm rope just shot through the belay device and was not able to be arrested. (Source: Edited from various reports sent in by Al Hospers)

INADEQUATE EQUIPMENT AND CLOTHING, INEXPERIENCE, DARKNESS, EXPOSURE
New Hampshire, Mount Washington, Damnation Gully

On a Tuesday morning in January, two ice climbers from Connecticut, Damian McDonald and Susanna Saarkangas (ages unknown), were rescued from the Alpine Garden above Damnation Gully on Mount Washington. They spent a night out in subzero temperatures and high winds. According to their own comments, they spent the night at the Harvard Cabin on Sunday night. They left the cabin at around 11 a.m. Monday to climb Damnation Gully.

According to the caretaker at the cabin, they were moving extremely slowly when he saw them on the second pitch of the gully at around 4 p.m. As they got to the top, the conditions had deteriorated significantly and it was dark. They did not descend the gully because the second had never rappelled before. Unable to traverse to the Escape Hatch, they huddled by a cairn near the Nelson Crag, eventually building a small snow cave and stomping around to keep warm.

The caretaker notified the authorities that they had not returned. The snow rangers got notification at about 10 p.m. Conditions at this time were -6 F with 70 mph wind gusts. A team of approximately 20 searchers went out at 6 a.m., some up Lions Head, some into Huntington, and some on the Auto Road. At this time temps were -17 F and wind gusts were 80 mph with fog and blowing snow. About 9 a.m., the climbers were spotted above Central Gully and were found by members of the MRS and AVSAR. They were led to the Auto Road where a snowcat took them to a waiting ambulance and the hospital in Berlin where they were treated for hypothermia and frostbite. They were expected to recover fully.

Analysis

The leader had done the climb before, but this was to be his partner's first climb. They were unprepared to spend a night out and, according to one report, had neglected to check the weather prediction for the day. (Edited from *The White Mountain Report*, January 27, 2005)

FALLING OBJECT—DEAD TREE (DISLODGED BY OTHER CLIMBERS)
New Hampshire, Whitehorse Ledge

On an early Sunday morning in August, I went out with two teenage clients with a plan to climb Standard Route to the Lunch Ledge via the Toilet Bowl and Crystal Pocket. We arrived at the Launching Pad around 8:30 a.m. There was a party already on the second pitch of Wavelength. I finished setting up the starting belay when another party consisting of two women came up. Their plan was to do the same route as us, but they decided to do the easy traverse 70 feet right to the Slabs Direct second anchor. Somewhere around this time I happened to notice that the upper group was on the Wavelength/Sliding Board dike.

Our two groups continued up parallel tracks until we were at the Crystal Pocket and they were at the second Slabs Direct anchor. My kids were climbing great and having a good time for their first time on a multi-pitch climb. In addition, it looked as if the potentially inclement weather wasn't going to be a problem. There was a lot of banter back and forth between our two groups and the other leader took some pictures of us.

The leader of the female party climbed up the crux steep slab, off their belay, clipped into a fixed piece, and padded up another 20 feet on the moderate slab. I was just getting ready to lead my next pitch when I heard a scraping noise from above and looked up in time to see what appeared to be a huge rotten-looking tree slide over the upper headwall just left of the Standard Route belay tree. I pushed my young clients into the belay and covered them with my body while repeatedly calling, "Rock," as loud as I could. Glancing right, I saw the female leader take a few steps to the left and her belayer huddle at the belay. The tree trunk broke into two sections as it went over the headwall and instantly fell very rapidly. I watched as it missed the leader but struck her belayer in the head! She was shock-loaded against the belay and lay there not moving.

I quickly called to the leader and determined that she was untouched and stable where she was. Calling to the belayer I received no answer. I then heard shouts from the ground, somewhere over near Sea Of Holes. They asked if everyone was OK. I told them NO, someone was injured and to call 911 and the Mountain Rescue Service. One of them took off running. While this was taking place, the leader repeatedly called down to her belayer, who was not moving or responding. At this time I truly feared the worst.

Amazingly, all this time my young charges did not panic or become emotional. I spoke calmly to the leader making sure she could stay where she was as at this time I believed that she was almost assuredly not on belay. She responded that she was fine and that she could possibly down-climb the 20 feet to the fixed protection. I asked her to stay put for a while longer. I decided that I could use one of my 60-meter ropes and tension-rappel to the injured belayer who was 50 feet below me and 40 feet to my right. I began to set up the belay and arranged for one of my young clients to simultaneously belay me on the other rope. Around this time, the person who had gone for help returned and started up Slabs Direct.

After repeated calls to the second, she finally responded weakly. I asked her if she could tie off her leader. She made a response I could not understand, but from what I could see, she did it. The leader then down-climbed to the bolt and clipped herself in. I kept looking up to see if anything else was coming down from the top of the cliff and thankfully at no time did any more debris appear. Just before I left my belay, I explained to my kids exactly what I was going to do and repeatedly told them both not to touch anything. Had they become emotional, I'm not sure I would have been able to do what I felt I had to do.

I carefully rapped down and tensioned over, reaching the injured belayer's position and clipping into her belay. I immediately noticed several things. There was reddish rotten bark all over the place, blood was on the rock near the belay and some of the gear, and a locking 'biner on the far-rightmost bolt was broken almost in half!

I spoke with her and was very happy to find that she was oriented and responsive. In the accident she had lost her glasses and was unable to see anything without them, which was disorienting to her. Stabilizing her head, I carefully checked her neck, spine, and extremities. Thankfully she had feeling in all areas. There was rotten bark on the back left side of her helmet where the tree trunk had struck her. She had a significant cut behind her left ear, numerous scratches and small cuts, and an extremely bruised but unbroken right thumb. For the first time since the accident started, I actually had a feeling that all of this was going to be OK.

I took the leader off the original belay and put her on my device. I then asked her to set herself up for a lower. I figured that would be easier for her than trying to untie and do a rappel. She did it and I lowered her to the anchor and clipped her in. Finally I knew that we were all reasonably safe. Around this time I realized that the weather was not going to hold. Clouds were building up in the Valley and every once in a while I could feel a sprinkle. As we were 200 feet up on a slab route with minimal available protection, it would not have been easy for other rescuers to get to us without hiking to the top of the cliff and rappelling 600 plus feet. I felt that, if at all possible, I needed to get the injured woman to the ground before things deteriorated. Of course, through all this, I was talking to my young clients, who were doing fine.

By now the climbers who had called for assistance, Rob and Mike, were heading up to the first belay on Slabs Direct and the Fire Department rescue people were on the scene. I explained that I wanted to lower both women to the Toilet Bowl anchor 150 feet down and 40 feet to the climbers-left of us. I spidered the injured woman to her partner and set them up to be lowered.

I put a second 'biner in the belay system to slow things down and hooked up an autoblock for security. Before I started the lower, I made myself slow down and make certain that absolutely everything was being done properly. I could feel my heart beating fast and my mind was working overtime. Rob brought Mike up to his belay on the pitch below us and immediately headed over to the Toilet Bowl just as I started lowering. They arrived at roughly the same time and all clipped into the two-bolt anchor. Of course by now it had started to rain! Why was I not surprised?

Somewhere around this time Joe K, a member of the Mountain Rescue Service team, had arrived at Lunch Ledge. That made me feel better. Once I was confident the lowered party were safely hooked in, I disconnected their ropes from my belay and dropped them. Rob and the female leader set up the second lower and began the process. Joe collected them at the Lunch Ledge and lowered them into the hands of the waiting EMT team where the injured party was whisked off to Memorial Hospital.

Now it was really pouring down rain. Fortunately it was warm rain and there was no thunder and lightning. I cleaned up the belay, made sure that my kids had me on belay again, and lowered myself off my belay. I quickly bat-manned and self-belayed back up to the kids where I immediately slowed things back down. I pulled my rappel rope and reset for a rappel. Putting the kids on a spider on me, I carefully rappelled first to the Toilet Bowl and then the Launching Pad then continued down to the ground. WHEW, we were all happy to be there.

We headed back to the parking lot, pausing to let Rob and Mike know how much their help had been appreciated. Another MRS member mentioned that they spoke to the party who had been on Wavelength and they admitted that they had accidentally dislodged the tree. I would really like to talk with them if at all possible so I can understand where they were and what took place. There is no blame here, just a search for knowledge!

Later that afternoon my son Daz and I stopped by the hospital so see how things were going. I was very happy to find that the injured party was doing very well and would have no lasting problems. She assured me that it was only going to be a short time before she was back on the rock. We were all very fortunate that, in spite of the injury, things worked out as well as they did. It was lucky that the leader was not knocked off the climb, the belayer was not seriously injured, the tree was rotten and not solid, the weather wasn't all that good so there weren't any other people on the cliff, my young charges and I were not in the path of the tree, Rob and Mike were nearby and able to help out, the EMT's and MRS got there very quickly, and there wasn't a thunderstorm. (Source: Al Hospers and a few details edited from the White Mountain Report)

(Editor's Note: This lengthy narrative is included because it provides some good lessons in how to manage a situation that could easily have taken a turn for the worse. Helmets off to the guide, those who aided in the rescue, the climbers directly involved, and the clients!)

WEATHER—WIND, FALL ON SNOW/ICE
New Hampshire, Mount Washington, Odell Gully

On December 4, a climber was traversing into the center of Odell Gully with his two partners. They were about a third of the way across the neck of the gully when a gust blew the lead climber off his feet and spun him, causing him to strike his face on the ice. He slid 400 feet down-slope on windslab and boilerplate and did not self-arrest because of being in a state of shock from the blow he experienced. He slid into rocks and stopped. His partners down-climbed to him, tied him in, and lowered him to more moderate terrain. One of his partners then went to call for help from Harvard cabin.

Analysis

The climbers were unroped but were planning on roping up when they reached technical terrain. The avalanche conditions were posted as "considerable" at the time. None of the party members had avalanche training nor were they equipped with beacons or the like. No party members were wearing helmets. They had not climbed together before. The leader/patient has 12 years ice climbing experience in Quebec, mostly on steep ice, but lots of time on Mount Washington and similar alpine climbs. The other climbers were similarly experienced.

The patient had no brain trauma and only sprains of both ankles (mild). His nose was broken with underlying ethmoid bone fractures that sent thin bone chips into both frontal sinuses. He had a displaced, open fracture of his L radius with associated comminuted (aka pulverized) fracture of his L elbow (olecronon) and an elbow dislocation. He had a fractured R elbow without dislocation and finally a rare anterior left shoulder dislocation. He spent until 4:00 a.m. in the operating room having these pinned, aligned, etc. He was released the next afternoon. This was only possible due to the fact that he luckily had no visceral injuries and no cardiopulmonary trauma. (Source: Brian Irwin)

FALLING ROCK—BLOCK PULLED OFF
New Mexico, Sandia Mountain Wilderness, Hail Peak

After breakfast and coffee, Sinjin Eberle and I set out to have a nice day for a multi-pitch 5.8 climb of Hail Peak on May 9, Mother's Day. The weather was warm and stable with a storm possibly moving in later that evening. The Sandias typically keep many climbers away because of the long approach times and thick raspberry and oak groves. We got an early start and planned to be off the climb by mid afternoon with only a moderate pace. As many climbers in the Sandias can attest, the old granite is great to climb, but the amount of loose rock is a major drawback, especially on approaches to many areas. The primitive approach to Hail Peak is no exception, with a two-hour fourth and fifth class terraced traverse that steadily gains exposure as Echo Canyon drops below. I had just scrambled my way up some loose blocks and saw Sinjin about 40 meters behind so as to not risk getting hit by rock fall.

Sinjin asked, "How does it look?"

"O.K., as long as you don't pull on anything too hard," I replied. Then all of a sudden I heard a quiet, "Oh… Marc…" I turned to look back and saw that Sinjin had pulled an incredibly large piece of granite loose. He lost his footing on the sandy slope, attempting to balance the rock back into position for enough time to escape its path. The boulder expanded from the face and first crushed onto Sinjin's hands, then it rolled on top of him. I tried to tell him to jump (out of the way), but it was clear that I was getting ready to watch a friend die. All I could see of Sinjin was from the middle of his shins down and the top of his head. The rock covered the rest of his body and was dragging him down the slope I had just crossed.

The ledge was only two to three meters wide that ended abruptly with some yuccas and a 50-meter cliff. Somehow, with the inertia of the rock (250-300 kg) and all of his strength, Sinjin was able to get the rock off of himself, but not before it clipped him in the back of the head, throwing him around like a rag doll. Blood was flying in the air from his crushed hands and torn open leg. I yelled at him to not move as he could have easily rolled once and gone the distance. He managed to hook a foot on a bush and maintain his position, as he was still remarkably responsive.

I have seen a lot of trauma from ten-plus years of EMS and I could tell already that the extent of his injuries would need a trauma center. Fortunately, I had brought a cell phone. With one hand I was calling a friend from the Mountain Rescue team and with the other I was setting an anchor so I could lower Sinjin off the rock. I called Steve Attaway.

"Steve, how are you?"

He knew me right away. "Good, how are you?"

"Fine, but Sinjin needs a helicopter to the West Face of Hail Peak, he's been crushed by a rock."

"O.K., see ya soon."

Steve knew the situation was critical and didn't dally around with details. He knew the right people to call at the New Mexico State Police and he immediately got the rescue team in motion. The call was short, but it was all that was needed and I had to save my phone battery for later. Meanwhile, I managed to assess Sinjin and see that his hands were crushed, bleeding, and useless to him. His leg was split open at the shin but not obviously broken, although he could bear a little weight and had numbness in his right foot. But perhaps worse were his arms and neck that were severely bruised. Crush-syndrome could easily ensue from the mechanism of injury, and organ failure was a real possibility. He was also facing the permanent loss of his hands or arms and major lifestyle changes.

We did all the medical care we could with a sparse first aid kit and then got him ready for a long lower. I could not do a standard pick-off because the only anchor was questionable at best and I had to back it up with my own body weight. So, after determining Sinjin most likely did not have a dangerous spinal injury, it was necessary to lower him off the ledge for a rescue team to gain access to him. Sinjin became courageous enough to be lowered off the cliff and was able to maintain most of his weight on one foot until he reached the bottom. Although he could manage this, he could not walk, and attempting to do so would exacerbate the situation. All fours were needed to get out of the canyon and Sinjin had maybe one -and-a-half at best.

Hours later, Jen Semon and Steve arrived with a rescue medical kit and we gave Sinjin a desperately needed IV and narcotics. Moments after that, Kirtland Air Force Base arrived with a CH-53 helicopter carrying a Para-rescue team. The winds were shifty at about ten to fifteen knots, but the down draft in that little vertical canyon made it seem like a hurricane. Sinjin was lifted by winch at a 35–40 degree angle with a tag line and taken to the hospital.

A ground rescue for Sinjin would have been complicated and absolutely would have taken into the next day. The storm that came in an hour after the rescue had gale forces that would have made it impossible for the CH-53. This would have proven a bad outcome for his medical well-being as he would have most likely lost a major portion of his hands and possibly his foot, secondary to infection and sepsis. He spent an extra two hours in surgery to make his hands functional again.

Analysis

What I learned out of this experience is that good decision making, being prepared, being lucky, and having good, fast connections all come together to escape disaster. Sometimes a safer route cannot be taken, so it is important to realize when the danger zone is present. It was a humbling experience for both of us to find ourselves at the mercy of nature, especially given the many years of climbing experience we have between us. (Source: Marc Beverly, Albuquerque Mountain Rescue, PA-C/Paramedic, and AMGA Certified Rock Guide)

VARIOUS FALLS ON ROCK, PROTECTION PULLING, FALLING ROCK, INADEQUATE PROTECTION
New York, Shawangunks

In 2005 there were 14 climbing accident reports, two of which were bouldering falls. Ten of the incidents occurred while ascending. Individuals fell, and six of the falls were made worse as a result of no or inadequate protection. There was one rappel incident in which the climber rappelled off the end of his rope, and there was one incident in which the climber had untied the rope before down-climbing. He fell 15 feet. Another climber tumbled over backward while trying to pull down a stuck rope. He dislocated his shoulder.

The average age of the climbers involved was 37, the average difficulty of the climbs was 5.6, and the average level of experience was moderate to experienced, with only two having little or no experience.

Not counted in the data were two snake bite events, one in which the climber was bitten with no consequence. (Source: From reports submitted by the Mohonk Preserve)

RAPPEL ERROR—FAILURE TO CHECK ANCHOR, INADEQUATE PROTECTION
North Carolina, Shiprock, Hindu Kush

On July 3, Lewis M. Jones II (22), and his partner, Joe Wilson (23) climbed Hindu Kush (5.8), a popular Shiprock route. Shiprock is a popular climbing area located in the Grandfather Mountain Corridor area of the Blue Ridge Parkway. After completing the climb, the pair decided to rappel down to their gear rather than hike back down to the base of the cliff. According to Wilson, they threaded their ropes through the anchors and threw the ropes down one by one. Wilson said when Jones attached himself into the rope via his ATC, he was above the anchors, so he moved to one side and lowered himself to a position below the anchors to begin his rappel. Jones leaned back to rappel and to Wilson's disbelief, he heard Jones yell and saw him fall approximately 100 feet to the ground.

Wilson ran over to the nearby trail that led down to the Rough Ridge parking area, located a hiker with a cell phone, and called EMS. After making the call, he made his way back to Jones. Upon reaching him, Wilson rolled him over to check his pulse and received no response. Evidently, Jones died instantly after hitting the boulders below. EMS arrived shortly thereafter.

Linville Central Rescue and Linville VFD members attached Jones to a defibrillator but were unable to revive him. He was transported to Watauga Medical Center in Boone, NC.
Analysis:
The accident was investigated by National Park Service and Linville Rescue personnel. When topping out Hindu Kush, the first set of anchors which can

be seen are those on the aid line, the Odyssey (to the east atop the prow that contains the climb Castaway). While the anchors on Boardwalk are much closer to the standard rappel route, they are obscured from view when finishing Hindu Kush. Lewis and Jones moved over to the Odyssey and set up their rappel through a pair of super-shut anchors, which allow the rope to be clipped directly into the shut rather than threaded through. Both climbers held an end of rope and dropped them to the ground. Jones placed himself on rappel while still on top of the cliff. Somehow in the process of lowering onto the anchors, the rope between the shuts and the climber clipped itself through the shuts, resulting in a bight of rope threaded through both shuts. Apparently Lewis was unaware of this happening. As Lewis eased his weight onto the anchors to get below them, the bight of rope slid through both anchors resulting in the accident. The investigation revealed that the gates of the super-shut anchors played a role in holding weight, as they were bent outward from the main axis of the equipment, suggesting that they were loaded by Lewis' body weight as he began to rappel.

An approaching storm may also have been a factor in the retreat chosen by the climbers.

A number of common practices could have been considered: 1) Attach to the anchors via a daisy chain or sling, down-climb to a point below the anchors, and then go on rappel; 2) before going on rappel attach an autoblock, prussik, or similar knot on the rope and attach to the harness, followed by placing a properly threaded rappel device above the pre-placed friction knot; 3) the climbers could have chosen to walk-off the climb, especially if incoming weather was a concern; 4) have your partner check the anchor and rappel setup before going on rappel. (Source: *Watauga Democrat*, July 6, 2005; Anthony Love, from a posting on carolinaclimbers.org on July 8; and Aram Attarian)

FALL ON ROCK, RAPPEL ERROR—RAPPELLING TOO FAST, INEXPERIENCE
North Carolina, Great Smokey Mountain National Park

Around 2:30 p.m. on July 25, Adam Holenberg (23) was rappelling from a cliff above Rainbow Falls in the Cherokee Orchard area when he fell approximately 30 feet, sustaining serious injuries. Holenberg had hiked three miles in to the falls, scrambled to the top, then solo rappelled down the face of the 80-foot-high cliff. He was using a very small (9 mm diameter) rope with an anchor and a figure-eight descending device. Witnesses said that he took very long bounds down the cliff, shock-loading the system, and that he was two-thirds of the way down the cliff when the rope severed and he fell about 30 feet to the boulder field at the bottom of the cliff. Bystanders called via cell phone for assistance.

Rangers arrived on scene by 5:00 p.m. Park medics stabilized Holen-berg and the rescue team conducted a semi-technical rescue operation to remove him from the boulder field and get him down to the trail surface. He was then evacuated by wheeled litter to an ambulance at the trailhead, transferred to a medical helicopter, and flown to the UT Medical Center in Knoxville. Holenberg suffered a fractured femur, fractured vertebra in the lower back, and a fractured wrist.

Analysis

The investigation revealed that the rope was military surplus Kevlar material and that there was a melted/frayed cut where it crossed over a sharp rock edge during Holenberg's rappel.

There is no indication that the victim was an experienced or even a novice climber. Each year we report on rappelling incidents such as this in hopes that the word will get out regarding proper technique for rappelling—even for those who only want to engage in this aspect of the sport of climbing. (Sources: Rick Brown, District Ranger, and Jed Williamson)

AVALANCHE—DID NOT READ PUBLISHED AVALANCHE WARNING, WEATHER, POOR POSITION, FAILURE TO FOLLOW INSTINCTS (ONE CLIMBER), CARRIED BEACONS—BUT NOT TURNED ON
Oregon, North Sister

We departed the Pole Creek Trailhead, 5,200 feet, at 1:00 a.m. on May 22 with the intent to climb North Sister via the Early Morning Couloir in a day. We arrived at 8,500 feet below the Northeast Face in four hours, five miles from the trailhead. We took a long 1½ hour break to evaluate the atmospheric conditions as we had experienced intermittent precipitation and variable cloud cover on the approach. The clouds showed no signs of building.

At 6:45 a.m. we departed and climbed the Northeast Ridge separating the Early Morning Couloir and the Villard Glacier routes gaining the North Ridge by 9:00 a.m. Of particular interest was the change in snow condi-tions; a good bucket step was typical on the east side. However, we found a solid but breakable crust on the west-facing slopes. We summited at 10:15 a.m. Conditions were still variable with the cloud cover decreasing and the ambient air temperature increasing.

The three viable descent options included the standard route on the southwest side of the mountain, our ascent route, or the Thayer Glacier Headwall route on the East Face of the mountain. Due to the time of day, the warming temperatures, and unfamiliarity with the snow conditions on the Southwest side of the mountain, we elected to descend the Thayer Glacier Headwall route. James Brewer and David Byrne had attempted the route the previous year and were familiar with the lower sections. Additionally, we observed that another team had just ascended and descended the route.

The ropes came out and we set up a rappel from Prouty Pinnacle. We had completed our rappel by noon and descended unroped. The snow conditions had become soft as we plunge-stepped our way down, sometimes up to our mid shins. The temperature was continuing to rise, especially on our descent route, which doglegs to skiers left around 9,400 feet. From there it is roughly 700 feet to the top of the steepest part of the route around 8,800 feet. David Byrne had arrived at 8,800 feet with James Ellers approximately 150 feet above, Nancy Miller approximately 150 feet above James Ellers, and James Brewer approximately 150 feet above Nancy Miller, all on skier's right of the main gully. David Byrne had just placed a rappel anchor when James Brewer yelled, "Slough!" then, "Avalanche!" in the same breath. A point release slide started above James Brewer, above the dogleg, and instantly grew in volume in both width and depth as it entrained the loose snow in its path. It missed James Brewer but swept James Ellers and Nancy Miller from their stances, despite their attempts at self-arrest once the slide overcame their positions.

David Byrne, who was toed in and looking up slope, was able to move up and out of the gully. James Brewer and David Byrne watched the deposition zone fan out 700 feet below for clues. Both James Ellers and Nancy Miller were observed in the debris fan. James Brewer and David Byrne connected at 8,800 feet and contacted 911 using a cell phone at 1:10 p.m. to request SAR mobilization. James Brewer and David Byrne called out to their partners and then began rappelling and down-climbing via slopes to skier's left of the main gully. Nancy Miller, who had the highest position in the debris fan, was reached in approximately 30 minutes. Nancy Miller provided a detailed assessment of her condition and information was relayed to authorities: critical conditions, including broken vertebrae, a compound fracture of the left wrist, several pelvic bone breaks, a dislocated right shoulder, and a broken left clavicle. James Brewer moved down to James Ellers, who had fractures to both lower legs, plus soft tissue damage. (It is important to note that both climbers continued to swim out of the debris once the debris fan reached less steep terrain.)

Efforts were made to provide first aid and comfort to James Ellers and Nancy Miller until the Camp Sherman Hasty Team arrived at 3:30 p.m. Shortly thereafter, additional Deschutes SAR members arrived on the scene with the assistance of the Oregon National Guard. James Ellers and Nancy Miller were packaged and air lifted to Sisters, where they were then transferred to the hospital in Bend. Thanks to the efficiencies of the SAR groups, all team members and rescue personnel were off the mountain by 6:30 p.m.

Analysis

James Brewer (51), David Byrne (38), James Ellers (36), and Nancy Miller (40) have been climbing together for over seven years, primarily in the Cascades and on trips to Canada, Alaska, Colorado, and Nepal. Each has at a minimum Level 1 Avalanche training and mountaineering first aid; James Brewer has WFR training.

Our experience humbled us all. Descending the Thayer Glacier Headwall route appeared to be the best decision based on what we knew at the time. In this case, it was elected as the quickest way down the mountain. It also avoided the longer and circuitous south- and west-facing slopes on the standard routes, which traverse several steep sections and under significant rime coated gendarmes and were receiving full sun. As is typical on the Cascade headwall routes, the angle varies between 40 to 50 degrees with some steeper sections. We assumed that the snow conditions on the headwall would be similar in character to the ascent route.

As we descended, we were alarmed by the speed at which the conditions were deteriorating. We knew we were out much later in the day than we had hoped. Our long early morning break certainly set us back, although we felt it was worth the wait to verify that the weather conditions were not worsening. As we worked our way down the headwall, we attempted to stay out of the gully and be aware of our surroundings. Fortunately James Brewer spotted the beginnings of the slide. His warning shout gave everyone a chance.

Out of common practice the avalanche forecast was checked on Thursday morning. No warnings posted at that time. We should have checked the avalanche forecast again on Friday but did not. We observed old slide debris on the mountain but saw no signs of recent slide activity. One team member later expressed that he had a strange feeling about the snow conditions on the ascent and, in hindsight, wished he had voiced this concern.

The slide that caught us had been triggered by a natural event. We carried our beacons on the climb but were not wearing them. Additionally, we were surprised by the amount of trauma that the slide caused to James Ellers and Nancy Miller. Providing the level of care necessary to treat the extensive injuries and subsequent evacuation would have required resources that are not carried into the mountains. Ingenuity would have been necessary were we in a remote location.

If we had not had the benefit of the SAR groups, the outcome most certainly would have been different. Many thanks to the Deschutes County Sheriff, Camp Sherman Hasty Team, the Oregon National Guard, and Deschutes Search and Rescue. (Source: David Byrne, with some additional information from Robert Speik)

FALLING ROCK, PROTECTION PULLED, INADEQUATE BELAY, OFF ROUTE

Oregon, Mount Washington

Mei Ding Stamplis (24) and husband Mathew Stamplis posted the following on a popular climber's Bulletin Board:

"We were on the North Ridge (July 2). Hadn't climbed it before and we got off route up at the summit pinnacle. Instead of directly climbing North Ridge, we traversed around it (climbers left) onto the east face. I could see a gully on the east face that looked climbable so we headed for that.

"The gully looked to be 4th class with some nasty exposure, so my wife belayed from below and off to the side. I went up about 20 feet and commented that there was no decent rock for placing pro. I finally settled on a large boulder (about the size of a person) that looked somewhat stable relative to everything else. I threw a sling around it and gave just a little tug on it and the whole thing just took off down the slope. It took a bad bounce and my wife couldn't get out of the way. She was struck on the shoulder and side of the head (helmet saved her life!). She fell off the ledge she was on and landed about 15 feet below on another ledge.

"If she hadn't landed on the ledge that she did (about three feet wide), there is no doubt we both would have been dragged right off the mountain (below us was 45 degree snow). She had set up a belay anchor but the anchor wasn't meant to take a load from that direction and didn't help at all to stop the fall.

"I was leading, she was belaying from below—there was nothing special about our setup. I did give the boulder a wiggle before I slung it and it seemed OK—it wasn't until it was slung and I gave it a slightly more firm pull that it gave loose."

Analysis

"In retrospect, the best thing we could have done was turn back and try another route after noticing the poor quality of the rock on the east face.

"But, assuming we were determined to climb where we did, the second thing we should have done is found a better spot for her to belay from. She was off to the side from where we expected any rockfall but, obviously, not far enough.

"Finally, given the big exposure on the east face, we definitely should have set up a bomber anchor for the belayer, something that would have kept her from falling after getting hit. The only anchor we had on belay was a sling around a horn, which was far from bomber.

"In short, our biggest mistake was simply not being able to properly evaluate the rockfall hazard. In our traverse around the pinnacle, we both noted that the rock was awfully crumbly. But we kept pushing on, hoping the rocks up the gully might be a little better."

FALL ON ROCK
Oregon, Three Fingered Jack

Kate Tinnesand (23), a graduate student at Oregon State University and member of Corvallis Mountain Rescue Unit, died in a fall while descending Three Fingered Jack, on July 23, after a climb with two other Unit members. They had completed the "technical" part of the climb, had unroped, and were working their way down the south ridge when Kate slipped on a gravel-covered ledge and tumbled over 700 feet on the west side of the mountain, sustaining fatal injuries.

Comment

She had been coming to CMRU meetings and training sessions since January and had just completed the interview process in June to become a full member. Kate enjoyed the outdoors including climbing the Cascade peaks in Oregon and Washington. Kate was finishing a Masters in microbiology and had aspiration to work as a climbing ranger in the parks. She will be sorely missed by all who knew her and especially her team in Corvallis. (Source: Rocky Henderson, Oregon Region MRA)

(Editor's Note: There was a fatality on Mount Hood's Cooper Spur route in the summer, but no details were sent forward. There have been 18 recorded fatalities on this route.)

FROSTBITE, OFF ROUTE, INADEQUATE FOOD, LOST EQUIPMENT
Washington, Mount Rainier National Park, Ptarmigan Ridge

On February 1, Chris Bamer (25) and Robert Montague (28) set out to ascend Ptarmigan Ridge. Both were guides for Rainier Mountaineering Incorporated (RMI). They expected to complete the climb by Thursday, but Bamer asked his girlfriend to call the NPS if the pair were not home by the evening of February 4. At 2015 on February 4, Bamer's girlfriend contacted Mount Rainier National Park and notified them of the ascent. Later that same evening, however, she received a cell phone call from Bamer during which he explained that he was okay but had a little frostbite on his hand and toes. Bamer stated that the route was quite icy and that they were taking longer than expected. They were camped near 12,500 feet, had plenty of fuel, and though they were low on food, they did not require assistance. This information was relayed to park officials.

At 0745 on February 5, Bamer called the NPS on his RMI radio and asked for climbing route directions across the summit and how to descend the Gibraltar Ledges route. The team was still camped at 12,500 feet and had to climb through the rocks near 12,800 feet before ascending to Liberty Cap. Bamer reported the frostbite but felt things were going to be okay. The team was encouraged to complete their ascent, as the clear weather was forecast to deteriorate. Bamer was asked to notify the NPS when they reached Liberty Cap (the false summit at 14,112 feet).

At 1444, Bamer called to say that the team had reached Liberty Cap and were making their way towards Columbia Crest. (Montague later stated that they were actually only at 13,200 feet when the call was made). At 1755, Bamer again called the NPS and reported that the team was somewhere between Russell Cliffs and Liberty Cap. They reported whiteout conditions, snowfall, and high winds; because of this, the pair elected to stop moving and set camp.

At roughly 1130 on Feb 6, Montague reported being in a steam cave on the summit. Their plan was to descend towards Gibraltar Rock and then to Camp Muir. He also reported on Bamer's frostbite, which included blackness in his toes and fingers and some blisters on his fingers. The team was in a snow cave on the summit and had run out of food and fuel. The wind was blowing 15mph and snow was falling.

Bamer and Montague left the summit at 1150 heading towards Gibraltar Rock. Along the way, they reported deteriorating weather conditions and numerous crevasses, reaching a rocky, corniced ridge at 1315. The team continued to descend, but the heavy snowfall and unfamiliarity with the route made route finding difficult. Over the next two hours, the pair tried to negotiate the Gibraltar Ledges but, in the end, had to rappel over some cliffs and descend steeper slopes towards the Nisqually Glacier.

The pair was in communication with the NPS throughout this process. NPS advised on route alternatives and predicted avalanche conditions. Bamer and Montague had difficulty with their GPS and compass. They reported very poor snow stability as they continued their descent.

Two rescue teams had been dispatched to Camp Muir earlier that day. The first team consisted of RMI guides Paul Maier and John Lucia, who arrived at Camp Muir around 1645 and, after a short break, continued toward the Nisqually Glacier to search for the pair. They reported dangerous avalanche conditions, low visibility, and heavy snowfall. They returned to Camp Muir at 1906 to get gear that would enable them to go out onto the glacier safely. A second team consisting of climbing rangers Stony Richards, Chad Kellogg, and Lara Kellogg arrived at Camp Muir at 1745 and then also headed out to search.

At 1817 Bamer and Montague experienced a small fall over steep terrain. They elected to cut their rope in order to get themselves out of their predicament. Montague lost his ice tools while digging himself out of the deep snow, which was over his head following the fall. They also lost a GPS and compass. Montague also reported that his headlamp was no longer working, and that the avalanche danger was extreme.

At about 1835, Bamer and Montague had regrouped and were descending once again. After about 30 minutes, they reported from 10,500 feet that the slope they were descending had become lower angle. At 2040, Kellogg, using a flash beacon, met up with Bamer and Montague at the 9,800-foot corner of the Nisqually and Muir Snowfield. Rangers Kellogg and Richards escorted them back to Camp Muir by 2130.

At Camp Muir the rescue teams provided food and medical care to the exhausted party. Bamer had not felt his feet for 36–48 hours. Many of his digits on both hands and feet were bruised to the first joint. The tips of his fingers and toes were purple and red. Blebs and blisters had already begun to appear on his hands. As transport would have to wait until the next morning, Bamer's extremities were dressed and packaged in anticipation of extraction and transport to a medical facility the next day. Montague was in good condition with no signs of frostbite.

The next morning Bamer was taken by helicopter from Camp Muir directly to Harborview Medical Center. Montague descended to Paradise with the team of rangers.

Analysis

Bamer and Montague set off expecting to complete their journey in three days with a fourth day for contingency. On the morning of the day they expected to be out they were only at 10,200 feet with all of the technical climbing still ahead. By evening they had ascended only another 1,200 vertical feet with more difficult climbing ahead. It may have been wise at some point during this day or even the previous one to reevaluate their plans in view of their slow progress, dwindling supplies, and the difficult conditions. A logical point for reevaluation would have been the base of the ice cliff at 10,500 on the ridge, as the more technical climbing begins at this point. Backing off the climb at this point would have been a tough decision for the pair having come this far and with their objective right before them. They would have already gained 7,000 feet with only 4,000 more to the summit.

On the other hand they had already used two-thirds of their planned time and they had not even begun the climb. There would have been little reason for the pair to presume the going would get any easier. If anything, the more technical terrain would likely slow the progress as they encountered the steeper ice pitches. On the morning of their fourth day, already out beyond their expected return, this was still a reasonable time for reevaluation of the feasibility of continuing the climb. At the rate they were climbing (1,200 feet/day) through the technical section they could have predicted that it would take them another two days to reach the summit. Even if they had to rappel several pitches to descend the technical climbing, it still would have taken less time and effort than continuing on. Descending would have also spared them from climbing through the questionable weather ahead. (Source: Mike Gauthier, Climbing Ranger)

WEATHER, EXHAUSTION, HYPOTHERMIA, INADEQUATE CLOTHING
Washington, Mount Rainier, Muir Snowfield

About mid-day on Saturday, May 2, Tim Stark (57) and his nephew Greg Stark (26) set out from the Paradise (5,440 feet) to Camp Muir (10,100 feet) planning to climb the Ingraham Direct route. When they set out, Camp Muir was visible from Paradise. By 1900, however, the entire route above 6,800 feet was in the fog, clouds, and snow. A party of two matching the description of Tim and Greg Stark were seen in the public shelter at Camp Muir. Independent climbers at Camp Muir said that this party left the shelter and descended shortly after they arrived around 1800. On the way down they got off route and descended onto the edge of the Paradise Glacier.

Either later that night or early on May 22 after trying to make camp and cook some food, they began their descent again but did not get far. Greg's backpack was left 50 yards from the camp. The tent was loosely strapped onto the back of Greg's backpack and the tent poles were partially collapsed. There was spilled food in the tent indicating the tent may have been packed in a hurry or that the weather was quite poor when they were packing up. Their sleeping bags were unpacked and loosely strapped onto the back of their backpacks. Neither Tim nor Greg was found with a map or a compass.

Tim's body was found approximately 100 yards from Greg's backpack and about 35 yards lower to the southeast. Tim was wearing four layers on his upper body, a pair of cotton pants, gaiters, plastic climbing boots, gloves, and a wool hat. Most of his clothing was appropriately synthetic. Tim was sitting on the snow with his feet pointed downhill. His backpack was still on his shoulders and his hands were in his lap. He was still wearing a headlamp. It was turned to the "on" position but was not shining.

Greg was found 175 yards from Tim and 100 yards lower on the glacier to the east. Greg was wearing a cotton button-down shirt as a base layer, a fleece sweater, a shell jacket and fleece gloves, canvas shorts, gaiters, and cross-training shoes. He was also seated on the snow. Over his wool hat he was wearing an LED headlamp, which was still on and shining dimly.

On Monday morning the Paradise climbing rangers' overdue report listed the Stark party. A check of the parking lot confirmed they had not yet returned. An intense investigation was initiated when Nancy Stark, Tim's wife, phoned to report that she had not heard from him. Climbing rangers Andy Anderson and Bree Lowen joined Pilot Doug Utech on an aerial search at about 1700. They spotted two inanimate individuals on the Paradise Glacier at 1830. Early the next day Rangers Anderson, Lowen, and Stefan Lofgren recovered the bodies from the glacier with the assistance of a helicopter piloted by Uttecht.

Analysis

Tim Stark had been to Camp Muir several times. When he and his nephew registered for their climb, rangers informed them of the inclement weather forecast for the duration of the weekend. Such weather is not uncommon for this time of year on Rainier. Over the course of the day the weather grew progressively worse. Climbing Ranger Mike Gauthier also on his way to Camp Muir that day recalls seeing the Starks and "leap-frogging" with them until about 1630 when he last saw them behind him still ascending into the cloudy and worsening weather just above Moon Rocks. By 1700 the winds increased to over 40 mph, it began to snow heavily and the visibility diminished to less than 100 feet. Two independent climbers staying in the public shelter reported seeing the Starks at Camp Muir around 1800. After finding out that the shelter was full, the Starks decided to descend around 1830 rather than set up their tent in the storm.

Ranger Gauthier began his descent from Camp Muir that evening at about 1915. He recalls keeping his head low and close to his body while following GPS coordinates to stay on the route as he descended. These conditions continued until just below 6,800 feet. He reported that the climb to Muir and back took twice as long as it normally takes him.

When the weather is like this, it is common for travelers on the Muir Snowfield to get pushed in the direction the wind is blowing (generally to the east.) Furthermore the descent route traverses mildly to the left. The combination makes it difficult to stay on route when there are no visual clues. The Stark's descent path seemed to have traversed left (east) under Anvil Rock and out onto the Paradise Glacier where they were found.

In the storm conditions things that are normally easy become challenging and challenging tasks become exhausting. The Starks must have worked extremely hard to get themselves along with all of their gear up to Camp Muir and would have been quite tired by the time they got there. The temperature and winds steadily worsened as they hiked up as well. While they were hiking they would have stayed warm because they were exerting a good deal of energy, but as soon as they stopped, they would have cooled off rapidly. Faced with poor conditions and a full public shelter, the thought of setting up their tent and spending the night in it in the storm must have sounded unappealing. Choosing to descend in the storm when they were already wet and chilling down rapidly was decidedly a poor choice, but perhaps understandable when one adds in the exhaustion, probable dehydration, and perhaps even the first hints of hypothermia that would add confusion to their thinking.

The descent must have proved frightening when they realized they were lost and had no way of knowing which way to go in the whiteout conditions.

When lost, one's pace slows while trying to decide which way to go. Slowing down in such conditions would accelerate the onset of hypothermia. Hypothermia impairs one's ability to make rational decisions. With their predicament rapidly spiraling downward, and still facing extreme conditions, we begin to get a picture of how these two succumbed to the environment.

One may be tempted to make a pronouncement regarding what the Starks should have done or pick out mistakes that should have been avoided: their lack of map and compass, wearing cotton, their failure to set up their tent and stay put in their sleeping bags. What is hard to grasp is the ease with which each small error snowballs, eventually creating an untenable situation. And then, of course, the rational mind cannot comprehend what causes the hypothermic victim to do the irrational. (Source: Mike Gauthier, Climbing Ranger)

FALL ON SNOW—UNABLE TO SELF-ARREST
Washington, Mount Rainier, Gibraltar Ledges

On June 10 about 0600, Mike Beery (29) and Ryan Tillman were climbing the Gibraltar Ledges route on Mount Rainier. Having just exited the ledges and entered Gibraltar Chute, Beery, who was a few steps in front of his partner, fell. Tillman did not notice the fall until his partner slid by him. Tillman shouted as he watched his partner unsuccessfully attempt to self-arrest. Beery continued to slide down the 45-50° slope and over a small rock outcropping. At this point, Tillman lost sight of Beery, who tumbled some 900 vertical feet down the chute until he came to rest on the shallower slope below.

Tillman pulled out his cell phone and called his girlfriend, who then called 911. He then began his descent down Gibraltar Chute to look for Beery. Approximately 35 minutes later, having found several pieces of his partner's equipment strewn along the route, including his ice ax, Tillman found Beery lying face-down with his pack wrapped tightly around his neck. Tillman, an EMT, cut the pack loose and took Beery's vitals. At 0635 Tillman found no respirations but a weak pulse of about 35. Ten minutes later, when he could no longer detect a pulse, Tillman began CPR on Beery. He continued CPR until 0855 when climbing rangers Matt Hendrickson and Andy Winslow, who were on a routine patrol of the Ingraham Direct, arrived on scene and relieved him.

The rangers had descended to Camp Muir and then ascended the Nisqually Glacier with rescue equipment. Once on scene, Hendrickson checked vitals on Beery and found him to be pulseless, unresponsive, and not breathing. Beery had obvious signs of serious trauma and was bleeding from the head and ears and nose. At 0900, with the information provided by the rangers, Mount Rainier's medical control advised rangers to stop CPR and pronounced Beery deceased.

At this point the rangers' highest priority was getting Tillman out of the chute as rockfall had increased with the warmth of the day. They escorted him down 250 feet onto a rock spur. After Tillman was secured the rangers went back to package and fly Beery's body from the glacier via helicopter. Hendrickson and Winslow then escorted the exhausted Tillman back to Camp Muir. Tillman was then flown off the mountain.

Analysis

It is unlikely we will ever know what caused Beery's initial slip, but the firm early morning snow surface, which had not yet been softened by sunshine, made any self-arrest a difficult prospect. Beery and Tillman were unroped at the time of Beery's fall. Tillman stated afterward that they had elected to remain unroped while traversing the ledges because of the lack of available points of protection along the catwalk-like section of route. At the time, there were only a few inches of snow on the narrow loose path. Pickets or ice screws are generally un-placeable along this stretch of route except, perhaps, in winter. While rarely used, rock may afford some protection, but is limited by the overall poor and friable quality of the rock here. Tillman reported that he and Beery had agreed that they would rope up as soon as they left the ledges. The location from which Beery fell was right in the transition from ledge to chute. While it is possible that Tillman may have been able to arrest his partner's fall, had they been roped, a more likely scenario is that without protection, both climbers would have fallen to their deaths. (Source: Mike Gauthier, Climbing Ranger)

FALLING ROCK
Washington, Mount Rainier, Fuhrer Finger

At 0720 on June 29, while ascending Fuhrer Finger, Brian Benedict was hit by rockfall and sustained an open fracture of his tibia and fibula. Benedict was a client of a Rainier Mountaineering Incorporated (RMI) guided party led by Kurt Wedburg. Wedburg immediately reported the accident and notification was provided to Mount Rainier National Park. While Wedburg's party assessed, stabilized, and splinted Benedict's leg, climbing rangers made arrangements for air extrication. Simultaneously, three other RMI guides led by John Race left Camp Muir to rendezvous with Wedburg's team.

With Benedict unable to walk, Wedburg's party methodically lowered Benedict back down the Fuhrer Finger taking care to avoid further rockfall. Upon reaching approximately 9,300 feet on the Wilson Glacier, Race's team began improving an area to serve as an LZ for the helicopter extraction.

Around 1200, the patient arrived in the vicinity of the LZ. Fifteen minutes later a Bell 206 LIII arrived on scene with climbing ranger Bree aboard. Benedict was loaded into the aircraft and flown to Harborview Medical Center in Seattle.

Analysis

The Fuhrer Finger route on Mount Rainier is a prominent snow couloir with an hourglass funnel at around 10,500 feet that varies in width depending on time of year. These features, along with its south facing aspect, result in the prevalence of rockfall on the route. As one Mount Rainier climbing guidebook states, "Warmth also means rock-fall; the routes demand helmets and call for a true alpine start," and further admonishes to "move quickly, as rock-fall is present in the hourglass..." Unfortunately, caution and the appropriate tactics can only reduce objective dangers such as rockfall and not eliminate them altogether. Despite their early start, this group encountered rockfall early in the morning. There is also reason to believe that because the previous day's meltwater froze during the early morning hours, it may actually have induced rockfall due to the expansion (and therefore prying ability) of water as it turned to ice between rock. (See July 29 rockfall incident for more in-depth explanation.)

It is up to each climbing party to decide its level of acceptable risk of objective dangers and to attempt to minimize this danger by applying common climbing practices. Wedburg and his group responded to the accident in an efficient and intelligent way that allowed for maximum safety and a quick extrication of the injured climber. The additional help from Race and his crew further enhanced the rapidity with which the rescue was effected. (Source: Mike Gauthier, Climbing Ranger)

FALLING ICE
Washington, Mount Rainier, Kautz Glacier

On July 5 Jim Curnutt (46), was hit in the thigh by icefall while ascending the Kautz Glacier Route, sustaining a serious leg injury. Curnutt's teammates used a cell phone to notify the NPS and lowered him to a safer location to care for his injuries.

Climbing rangers Charlie Borgh and Tom Payne were climbing the Fuhrer Finger route when they were called to respond. The rangers were dispatched to the accident site where they provided emergency care and assessed the possibilities for air evacuation. The Oregon Army National Guard responded to the Park Service's request for a med-evac airship sending a Blackhawk helicopter from Salem. A paramedic was lowered via hoist to the 11,500-foot location in the Kautz Icefall. After triage, the patient was successfully lifted from the mountain and flown directly to Madigan Army Hospital for treatment.

Analysis
Rock and/or icefall are natural phenomena on every climbing route on Mount Rainier. Climbers are particularly vulnerable to falling ice in those areas where climbing routes traverse under or climb through active icefalls. The frequency at which seracs calve from an icefall appears not to be related to the time of day as one might easily assume. Icefall drones on continuously, albeit slowly, propelled by the unceasing downward pressure exerted by the mass of glacier above. Thus, one cannot avoid icefall even by climbing, for example, in the early morning hours. Noting icefall hazard zones and moving quickly through them can reduce the possibility of being hit, but short of not climbing, one cannot reduce the odds to zero. (Source: Mike Gauthier, Climbing Ranger)

TRIP/FALL ON SNOW—TWICE, UNABLE TO SELF-ARREST—FALL INTO CREVASSE
Washington, Mount Rainier, Ingraham Glacier
On July 7 at 0720, John Lucia (31), a guide with Rainier Mountaineering Incorporated (RMI), was leading a rope team up the Ingraham Glacier around 12,800 feet when one of the clients, Peter Bridgewater (54) fell on the icy slope. Lucia successfully arrested the client's fall and then attempted to place a picket for a running belay. After that, Lucia's memory becomes fuzzy, but he does recall wanting to put Bridgewater on a "short tie-in" as he was concerned about Bridgewater's footing. During this time, Bridgewater somewhat regained his footing and starting crawling towards Lucia. As he ascended, slack was created in the rope; moments later Bridgewater fell again and pulled Lucia off his feet. Lucia described being unable to self-arrest due to the momentum and the hard ice. The other two clients, Matt Fisher (42) and Patrick Clements (36), also attempted to self-arrest, but were subsequently pulled off as Bridgewater and Lucia slid by.

The team fell approximately 150 to 200 feet down the Ingraham Glacier before hitting a crevasse. Lucia and Bridgewater were tossed across this crevasse while Clements and Fisher fell into the crevasse and landed on a shelf 20 feet down. Lucia was knocked unconscious during the fall but regained consciousness shortly thereafter. Lucia, who sustained lacerations and a head injury, radioed for assistance to other RMI guides as he assessed the team's injuries.

The initial call to the Park Service indicated that all of the members of the team were badly hurt, including femur fractures, serious head injuries and spinal injuries. Within minutes of the initial call, climbing rangers Gauthier and Kessler had a rescue team on stand by ready for flight, while air support from the military was requested. A Hughes 500D helicopter that had just arrived at the park for material hauling was diverted for rescue operations.

While the carrying capacity of that ship was limited, the maneuverability and small footprint for landings made it extremely useful during the initial stages of the rescue.

At 0840 helicopter 12F, piloted by Jerry Grey, was launched to Camp Schurman to pick up climbing ranger Jeremy Shank and insert him on scene with rescue equipment. Ranger Matt Hendrickson at Kautz Helibase was flown to the accident scene on the second flight. Those rangers assisted Lucia and four other guides already on scene in extricating the injured clients from the crevasse. Shank and Hendrickson provided patient care and technical rope rigging skills.

Clements and Fisher, the two climbers in the crevasse, were the most critically injured. Clements had serious head, spinal and chest injuries in addition to a suspected broken femur. Fisher had sustained serious chest injuries with multiple rib fractures. Bridgewater, also banged up badly, sustained a dislocated shoulder. Bridgewater was ambulatory and therefore able to walk to the LZ. He was airlifted out when the next climbing ranger, David Gottlieb, arrived on scene in 12F. Gottlieb arrived at 1002 with additional rescue equipment; Bridgewater was flown to Kautz Helibase and met by medics and the NPS ambulance.

Rescuers continued stabilizing and packaging Clement and Fisher into litters for crevasse extrication. A 20-foot technical raise was needed to extricate Clement and Fisher from the crevasse before they could be hoisted from the mountain. At 1042 VIP Climbing Ranger Andy Winslow was flown to the scene and Lucia was then flown off the mountain to Kautz Helibase. Lucia and Bridgewater were transported to Tacoma General Hospital via AMR ambulance.

During this time, two Oregon National Guard Blackhawk med-evac helicopters and one Fort Lewis Army Reserve CH-47 Chinook helicopter arrived at Kautz Helibase. The crew of first Blackhawk enroute to the park was given GPS coordinates of the accident scene in order for them to complete a flyover and familiarize themselves with the site.

The field operations continued to prepare the remaining two patients for extrication. Raising the climbers from the crevasse was slightly hampered by an overhanging snow lip. As Clements was being raised to the surface, the first Blackhawk was launched to retrieve him via hoist. The ship arrived on scene 14 minutes later and inserted one medic with litter. That medic helped rangers to transfer the patient to the National Guard's litter before hoisting Clements into the ship at 1159. The ship flew directly to Madigan Hospital in Tacoma with the patient. Clements was the most critically injured of the four.

At 1233, minutes before the last of the injured was ready for airlift, the second med-evacked Blackhawk was launched from Kautz with an NPS medic (Rob Bjelland) onboard. A repeat of the previous operation was made to hoist Fisher from the accident site and fly him to Harborview Medical Center.

The RMI guides assisting with the rescue descended to Camp Muir after the patients were evacuated. The Army Reserve Chinook was launched at 1503 to retrieve the climbing rangers from the top of Disappointment Cleaver via Jungle Penetrator.

Lucia was released later that day after being treated for a broken orbit, lacerations, and contusions. Clements spent six days in the hospital having suffered two broken cervical vertebrae, six broken ribs, a ruptured spleen, severely bruised femur/thigh, broken nose, and serious facial lacerations. Fisher remained in the hospital for five days with six broken ribs, a punctured lung, and a lacerated liver. Bridgewater was released that day having been treated for a dislocated shoulder.

Analysis

One of the difficulties for a guide is the gamble of who will end up on your rope. While RMI clients are screened for fitness, those on the standard summit climbs are given only a few hours of technical training. A majority have never used an ice ax or crampons before. Clients are given specific instructions on what to do in the event of a fall, but a novice, especially when panicked, cannot be expected to react with rapid and correct reflexes. It seems Lucia, having successfully caught Bridgewater's first fall was formulating a plan to reduce the risk Bridgewater posed to his rope team when, only moments later, his client stumbled and fell again. Once pulled off his feet, Lucia stood little chance of arresting both his own fall and that of Bridgewater's on the early morning boilerplate surface. While experienced mountaineers observing the fall of rope team members upslope might be expected to drop into self-arrest, digging in his ice ax and front points vigorously in preparation for the impending shock load, little can be expected from those whose only experience with self-arrest is a few minutes of dropping onto flat ground from a standing positions without the realism of even a good tug on the rope. Given these imposed conditions, Lucia, it seems, did the very best he could. (Source: Mike Gauthier, Climbing Ranger)

(Editor's Note: Rangers and MRA personnel used a dynamometer to test the forces of snow anchor systems and human anchor systems—as in self-arrest—several summers ago on the Muir snowfield. Many were surprised to learn how quickly and easily belayers could be pulled from the self-arrest position, even when they were allowed to get into position prior to the climber simulating a fall.

Of note here is the hi-tech rescue that was accomplished. In earlier years – before cell phones and several available helicopters, the results of such an incident would likely have been quite different.)

OFF ROUTE, FALLING ROCK, FALL ON ROCK—RAPPEL ANCHOR FAILURE, INADEQUATE PROTECTION
Washington, North Cascades National Park, Sharkfin Tower

On July 10, a six-person team set out to climb Sharkfin Tower in North Cascades National Park. After a glacier crossing, the group passed the standard gully used to access the objective, the southeast ridge of the peak, and ascended a similar, but further gully. Realizing this, the group began a traverse in two rope teams of three, employing belays, to get back into position for the ridge climb. During this movement, rockfall struck one member, causing injuries to her face, eye, jaw, and one hand, but left her ambulatory with assistance. The group decided that rescue assistance would be necessary for evacuation of their injured member but planned to first retreat back down the gully they had ascended as a group to the top of the glacier. During this time the weather, which had been good at the start of the day, began deteriorating.

The group faced a descent of approximately 300 to 400 feet down a gully of mixed snow and rock. The plan was for two rappels, each using the group's two full ropes. A first anchor was constructed around a large rock sitting on a slab. Two climbers rappelled individually without incident to a point mid-gully, at which one began constructing the next anchor in the snow. The remaining four planned a descent involving two climbers rappelling on single strands of rope with the injured member connected closely by daisy chain to them so as to assist her descent. The fourth member would later rappel solo.

At mid-gully the first two heard the rappel commands from above, followed shortly by rock commotion, and made a quick observation of falling climbers with a tumbling rock before taking cover. Four climbers fell the entire gully-length to the top of the glacier. The two at mid-gully were not hit and down-climbed the steep snow to the glacier.

Three climbers died and the fourth sustained a serious head injury and was not conscious until hospitalization. One of the un-injured climbers went for help while the other stayed at the scene. A mountaineering guide was encountered in the basin and ascended with his cell phone and gear back to the scene. National Park Service officials were contacted by cell phone. By this time, it had begun to rain, complicating the effort to provide care at the scene and initiate a helicopter rescue from the ranger station. A team of rangers hiked through the night to reach the scene and at 7:00 a.m., a period of clearing allowed helicopter evacuations of the seriously injured climber directly to a Seattle hospital, the two uninjured climbers flown to the ranger station, and the three body recoveries completed.

Killed in the accident were Jo Backus (61), Mark Harrison (35), and John Augenstein (42). Survivors were Wayne McCourt (31) who was injured,

Janel Fox (28), and Mike Hannam (27). The most experienced and designated leaders of the group were Backus and Harrison. All had at least basic mountaineering experience here in the Cascades. There were no absolute novices, but I believe Fox and McCourt were under the "tutelage" of the leaders. My understanding from the survivors and friends/colleagues of the victims was that several of them, or all of the other four, had intermediate to advanced experience, with a range of Cascades ascents behind them. None of them climbed Sharkfin Tower previously.

Analysis

Route-finding. While a climb of Sharkfin Tower could certainly be made using the gully ascended by this group within reasonable daylight timeframes (the Sharkfin Tower ascent is much shorter in comparison to nearby North Cascade peaks), not taking the direct approach gully resulted in complications for this group, as being off-route often does. These included extending the travel time frame on a day of deteriorating weather (critical in the North Cascades) and providing further route-finding complications and exposure to technical terrain. The approach across the glacier through the gully and to the notch that begins the climb is entirely visible from the hike and campsite in lower Boston Basin. When this is possible, a team agreed-upon "visual fix" on preferred terrain and most efficient route can be useful in preventing later difficulties.

Initial rockfall. One survivor statement indicates that the initial rockfall that debilitated a member was party-induced, although this is not an entirely assured conclusion. At any rate, travel in areas of potentially loose rock demands a high degree of awareness of fellow climber's locations and movement, especially with larger party sizes. The analysis here should also show that all members of this team were wearing helmets and during this traverse seemed to be communicating about each team's position. The teams *were* attempting to take separate lines across the traverse, (which potentially raises the hazard); however, this party-inflicted rockfall was within one rope team.

Rappel anchor failure. Survivors described the rock anchor as "refrigerator-sized," that it was "tested" by efforts to kick and move the rock, and there was no recollection by survivors of any team member questioning the rock's integrity as an anchor.

Investigators estimated the size of a rock found at the gully's base believed to be the anchor at about 6 x 4 x 3 feet. The anchor was constructed with one cordelette and one webbing joined with a locking carabiner, as one anchor point, with no backup. This anchor rock was situated on a somewhat down-sloping slab surface of mixed rock and soil surrounded by small loose rocks. The two ropes were connected by a double fisherman's knot through the carabiner with stopper knots at each rope end. The combined weight of the three people rappelling together with packs was likely between 500–600 lbs. While it is impossible for any climbers to know definitively the exact force any selected anchor can hold, the tragic end to this event shows this weight was too much for this anchor. Statements and evidence indicate the anchor failure happened when the three were about ten feet into the rappel. The accident was compounded by the fourth member (meant to rappel last separately) being clipped to the anchor. Later observations of the area immediately around the anchor site showed few backup options, at least of the type and proximity that with the standard climbing gear available in the party's gear could have held the primary anchor in place. (Source: Kelly Bush, SAR Coordinator, North Cascades National Park)

FALL ON HARD SNOW–SLACK IN THE ROPE
Washington, Mount Rainier, Emmons Glacier

On July 12 at 1545, four members of a seven-person Mountaineers group, Chris Clapton, Rebekah Koch, Theresa Fielding, and Tom Labrie, were descending the Emmons on one rope when Koch caught a crampon on some rope slack and tripped at 13,500 feet. Her fall pulled Fielding and LaBrie off their feet, and the three began to tumble down the 40 degree icy slope. Clapton went into self arrest and caught the fall, preventing a much more significant accident from occurring.

Labrie broke his nose and injured his leg during the fall. Fielding severely sprained her ankle. Clapton and Koch secured the team with an anchor. The party's second rope team, which included party leader Doug Smart, descended to the accident site. They were joined by an unassociated climbing team of three who offered to help. After the injured were stabilized, the assisting party descended to seek more assistance for the injured.

Meanwhile, climbing rangers at Camp Schurman, using a spotting scope, had already observed the climbers gathering near 13,500 feet shortly after the accident. This gathering, considering the location and time of day, seemed to indicate trouble, so rangers continued to observe. At 1654, the rangers saw the group of three climbers leave the scene and descend the Emmons Glacier route. Now, convinced there was something amiss, Climbing Ranger Jeremy Shank and volunteer Mimi Allin quickly geared up and began to ascend the route. At 1732, Shank and Allin met a single member of the three-person team who had unroped and run down the Emmons to report the accident. That climber informed the rangers of the nature of the accident and the victims' injuries. Realizing that this situation would require more equipment than they had, Shank and Allin descended to Camp Schurman and prepared for a longer evacuation and possible overnight on the mountain.

At 1812, Rangers Shank and David Gottleib left Camp Schurman accompanied by Mount Rainier Alpine Guides Eric Stevenson and Dorja Sherpa. The four rescuers carried extensive overnight gear and medical equipment.

Around the same time, at the accident site, Smart chose to stay with LaBrie and Fielding. The three had a stove, shovel, parka and two sleeping bags (donated by the assisting party). Clapton then led the remainder of the group down the glacier back to their camp. Smart was unable to excavate a snowcave in the firm snow and use the stove, so the injured used the sleeping bags, while Smart wore the parka. The winds blew steady at 15-20 mph with higher gusts and below freezing temperatures. All three became hypothermic by the time the rescue party arrived at 2159.

The rescue team began clearing a site for tents and by 0015, the tents were erected and the guides departed back to Camp Schurman. The three hypothermic climbers were placed in a tent and rangers began administering hot water and food. It was a rough night. One of the tents partially collapsed under the wind and blowing snow as the temperatures dropped. At dawn, Gottlieb and Shank prepared the site and the patients for the helicopter extraction. The Oregon Army National Guard launched a Blackhawk helicopter from Salem, Oregon, at 0635 and was able to insert a medic on scene at 0757. By 0820, both patients had been hoisted aboard the ship, which then transported them directly to Memorial Hospital in Yakima.

The rangers descended the Emmons Glacier to Camp Schurman with Smart. Smart and the remaining members of his team then packed up their equipment and departed for White River.

Analysis

Several things could have turned from bad to worse on this incident. The original fall caused by slack in the rope generated enough force to knock two of the remaining team members off their feet. Thankfully, the rope leader was able to arrest the fall. Slack in the rope during glacier travel is not only dangerous because of the tripping potential, but also it allows the faller time to accelerate, thereby generating greater forces (shock load) on successive team members. Glacier travel, with its potential for crevasse falls, requires a snug rope between team members. Paying attention and communicating with your partners along with adjusting pace to keep the rope snug is critical.

The initial accident blossomed into other potentially dangerous incidents. Unroping and running solo down the Emmons Glacier late in the day to report the accident could have added yet another victim should that climber have ended up in a crevasse due to weakening snow bridges. It's important to resist the temptation to let urgency overpower good judgment.

By choosing to stay with Labrie and Fielding, Smart also became hypothermic. While one's intentions may be good, critically evaluating one's own ability to assist versus the possibility of becoming a liability must be considered carefully. Like the other climbers, Smart was tired after a long summit climb. In the end, he did not have the energy to erect a wind-break or fire up the stove and became a third victim in need of assistance.

Consideration was given to trying to hoist the patients off that evening, but given the technical nature of the terrain and the lack of experience of most paramedics in a technical alpine environment, it was determined that inserting a medic without mountaineering experience on the upper mountain would have set the scene for creating a fourth victim. The decision was made to wait until climbing rangers could secure the site and prepare for the hoist operation. (Source: Mike Gauthier, Climbing Ranger)

LOSS OF CONTROL—VOLUNTARY GLISSADE, IMPROPER USE OF CRAMPONS
Washington, Mount Rainier, Inter Glacier

On July 15 at 1348, the communication center notified Camp Schurman that a climber had broken his leg near the bottom of the Inter Glacier. Climbing rangers Chris Olson and Stoney Richards left Camp Schurman at 1415 arriving on scene at approximately 7,400 feet on the Inter Glacier 30 minutes later with a Cascade Litter.

Randy Kruschke (age unknown) had been glissading when his crampon caught an edge causing him to tumble and break his right tibia and fibula. Kruschke's teammates had already splinted his leg with a foam pad and ski pole and after quick evaluation of the injury, Olson elected not to re-splint the fracture to prevent further injury or delay. Olson and Richards packaged Kruschke into the litter and with the assistance of Kruschke's teammates lowered him to the base of the Inter Glacier where he was wheeled down to Glacier Basin. Kruschke was airlifted to the hospital from Glacier Basin

Analysis

Crampons are a great tool when on firm snow and ice but quickly become a hazard as the snow warms. Knowing when to use them and when to remove them—and then stopping at the appropriate time to make the change can lead to preventing this kind of accident. Novice climbers often mistakenly assume that they must wear crampons whenever on snow. It is hard to imagine a time when glissading with crampons would ever be considered a good idea.

Kruschke chose to leave his crampons on even though it was late in the day, the snow was soft, and he was glissading. In the classic fashion, when Kruschke picked up speed during his glissade, the rear tines of his right crampon snagged in the snow. This resulted in snapping the two bones (tib/fib) of his lower leg and throwing his body over his feet, sending him into an uncontrolled tumble. (Source: Mike Gauthier, Climbing Ranger)

FALLING ROCK HITS CLIMBER—DESPITE DOING ALL THE RIGHT THINGS
Washington, Mount Rainier, Disappointment Cleaver
On July 29, Estee Fernandez (29) was descending the base of the Disappointment Cleaver with her partner when a two-foot diameter rock hit her in the back, knocking her about ten feet down the slope. She and her partner walked to Camp Muir and contacted the guide service who then contacted the Park Service.

As there was a language barrier preventing good initial communication, the mechanism of injury became the deciding factor in evacuating Fernandez by air. A Bell 206 Long Ranger piloted by Doug Uttecht flew Climbing Ranger Andy Anderson to Camp Muir to pick up Fernandez who was loaded on a backboard and the two were flown directly to Harborview Medical Center.
Analysis
The Disappointment Cleaver is notorious for both natural and human-triggered rockfall. Fernandez and her partner were fairly experienced climbers from Spain. They were fit and knew that they could move fairly quickly on the route. Most parties leave from Camp Muir between midnight and 2 a.m. Often this will create a traffic jam on the route and cause people to stop in zones where rock and icefall are a hazard. Fernandez and Jon knew this and chose to leave later than most people at 2:30 a.m. to avoid the crowds. Fernandez and Jon climbed to the top of the Cleaver without running into any of the other parties. They caught up with and passed all of the other climbers between the top of the Cleaver and the summit. To stay ahead of the crowds, they descended quickly and well ahead of all of the other parties.

This accident illustrates that even when you make good decisions the mountains can be dangerous. Fernandez and her partner knew their fitness and skill levels well enough to determine their own safe time to depart rather than following the decision of the masses and ending up in a traffic jam. They had proper equipment and clothing, including helmets. They were traveling early in the day when natural rock and ice-fall are presumed less common. Fernandez said that they also had not exhausted themselves on the climb because they wanted to be alert and safe on the descent. Short of having lightning reflexes and being able to dodge a rock that is falling toward you from behind, there is not much more that these two could have done. Even after the accident they did the right thing: having determined that she could still move and not wanting to wait for help in an area proven to be a rockfall zone, Fernandez and her partner continued onto a safe place where they could get help.

Mount Rainier is not known for the high quality of its rock, but rather for the fine snow and ice that hold the volcanic rock in place. The common belief that natural rockfall is minimized by climbing early in the day when the snow and ice are holding the rocks together and meltwater is at a minimum appears to have some validity, but there are other factors to consider. One such factor is that water expands upon freezing. Since the coldest time of a 24-hour summer diurnal cycle is generally around 4 or 5:00 a.m., it stands to reason that water droplets behind rocks are as likely or more likely to undergo freezing at this time. The expansion forces of these crystals are known to be huge and doubtless they may pry rock and boulders from their perches. This may at least partially explain the common movement of rocks during the coldest time of day and the countless rockfall accidents that occur even in the wee hours of the morning. (Source: Mike Gauthier, Climbing Ranger)

(Editor's Note: Other incidents on Mount Rainier included the following: Three stranded climbers who were trying to travel light and fast, but who overestimated their skills and physical abilities. They exhausted themselves and had to seek help from the rangers. Two medical incidents, not included in the data, were a 39- year-old man who experienced torn chest muscles and a 52-year-old man who did not reveal a previous history of back problems. Rangers had to take them from high camp by sled.)

FALL ON ROCK, RAPPEL ERROR—RAPPELLED OFF END OF ROPE
Wyoming, Lander, Sinks Canyon

On May 4, Jim Ratz (52) fell to his death while rappelling from a route called Honeycomb, four miles from his home in Lander.

The following description and analysis were the result of careful investigation on the part of the individuals cited below.

The climbing area and route. Honeycomb (5.9+) is a climb in Sinks Canyon State Park on the first sandstone buttress on the north side of the mouth of Sinks Canyon near Lander, WY. The climb is approximately 160 feet from the base to the top. There is a rappel anchor approximately three quarters of the way up the climb (about 120 feet) on a sloping ledge that is almost a hanging belay. There is another ledge, about 60 feet up from the base of the cliff, that is beneath the honeycomb (most difficult) section of the climb, which we will refer to as the "lower ledge." The lower ledge is very large and flat.

The plan. Jim set out at noon to do some laps (cycles of climbing up and rappelling off) on Honeycomb and to scout a location to add a bolt to

This picture by John Gookin shows relative heights and lateral positioning, which is important to understanding why we think Jim intentionally went to the lower ledge.

make the move over the roof better protected. Jim had climbed Honeycomb many times before and had climbed it with clients. Jim planned to join Tom Hargis after this to do some other climbs together.

The fall. Jim was found lying on his back by Tom Hargis at the bottom of the climb. Jim probably fell around 3:00 p.m. Tom and a friend were on a climbing route just around the corner from Jim and were expecting him to join them after he did a few laps on Honeycomb. When they hadn't heard from Jim in a while, Tom went to check on him. Andy Blair was also there climbing and did CPR on Jim. Andy is a CPR Instructor, Wilderness EMT, and a first aid instructor for the Wilderness Medicine Institute of NOLS.

Analysis

The rappel and the origin of the fall. Jim's body was found 60 feet below the lower ledge and was close to the base of the cliff. This indicates that he fell from the area of the lower ledge. If he had fallen from higher up on the cliff, he likely would have hit the lower ledge during the fall. We (Hargis & Gookin) did not find blood anywhere on the cliff face. Deputy Coroner Bill Durnal also rappelled down the cliff face and couldn't find any blood.

When Jim switched to rappel, he needed to double his rope to make it retrievable. From the locked carabiners on his devices, we infer that Jim was using both devices (Reverso and autoblock) on the descent shortly before he fell, and that he rappelled to the end of the rope, which went to the lower ledge. The final position of the rope also indicates that he was at the lower ledge rather than the usual semi-hanging belay station that exists 87 feet above.

Position prior to fall. The greatest mystery is why Jim was on or near the lower ledge, but this fact is clearly established by his equipment and by his impact site. This is too far below the rappel station to be consistent with a momentary lapse in attention, since he had to rappel over a roof to get there, and he had to intentionally traverse right to get the rope in the crack where it remained.

One end of his doubled rappel rope was 8–10 feet longer than the other and he was at or near the end of one strand. When rappelling on a Reverso, the lack of rope-weight at the tail end makes it noticeably more difficult to brake the rappel.

The Equipment

The rope. He was using a new 60 m x 10.5 mm semi-dynamic, low-stretch climbing gym rope. (Jim measured this new rope at the NOLS Rocky Mountain equipment room two days before the incident and it measured 1.5 meters longer than 60 meters.) Rob Hess, co-owner of Jackson Hole Mountain Guides, says that new ropes are generally cut a little long while under tension, but that they quickly shorten to the marketed length upon use. This rope was brand new. It was not marked in the middle.

Jim's rope was found threaded through the two Metolius rap-hangers at the top of Honeycomb. The rap-hangers are larger than most bolt hangers specifically so you can thread a rappel rope directly through them without the need for a carabiner that would be left behind, but they have more rope drag than a carabiner does because of the sharper rope bend radius.

The rope was rigged for a pull-down rappel. When climbers rappel off Honeycomb and use the typical sloped belay station, there is considerable rope drag when trying to pull the anchor through the Metolius rap-hangers. When we re-rigged the rope, we were able to pull it (from the lower ledge) through the hangers with a moderate two-handed effort, but it also got caught easily and stuck in the vertical crack above the lower ledge.

Someone had pulled Jim's rope from the climb before we could inspect it in situ, but we do have a photograph taken before it was removed. The placement of the bottom of the rope indicated that Jim had been on the lower ledge beneath the rappel station. This is because the rope was pulled approximately ten to fifteen feet to the right side (looking up) of the natural fall line and was lying in a crack above the actual Honeycomb section of the climb.

One end of the rope stopped on the lower ledge. Another end went about ten feet below that ledge. One probable reason for this unevenness was because, as stated earlier, the middle of the rope was not marked. There was no knot in the end of the rope. Some climbing partners of Jim said that he wouldn't have knotted the rope in this situation because of the high potential to get the rope hung up in the cracks on that rappel.

The "Reverso" belay/rappel device. The device had a single *locked* Metolius Matrix carabiner. The fact that the carabiner was still locked indicated that he had rappelled through the end of the rope

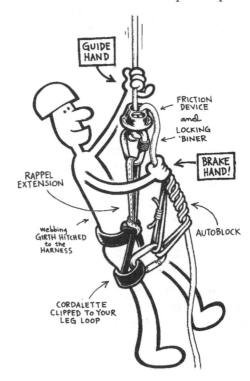

This illustration by Mike Clelland shows one correct arrangement of a belay/rappel device and autoblock backup hitch. Jim chose to use a Reverso, but was not using an extension sling.

rather than unclipping from the rope. Jim typically used two carabiners for more rope drag while using thinner ropes. He had one carabiner rigged into the Reverso; the other was clipped on his harness but not clipped into the Reverso, which makes sense, since he was rappelling on a double strand of a slightly fatter rope (10.5mm) than usual.

The autoblock loop. The loop was long enough that if Jim's body rotated it could bump his Reverso, rendering both the Reverso and the autoblock hitch ineffective, which could have triggered a rapid descent. To do this would require lifting and rotating his right leg inward. Jim had low speed abrasions on his right posterior: these marks support a scenario where a slip pushed his right leg forward and up, moving the autoblock towards the Reverso.

The carabiner was locked on his autoblock, indicating that it too had last been in use until reaching the end of the rope rather than being unclipped. (His climbing partners say he would have routinely left the carabiner gates unlocked if he unclipped them, because an unlocked carabiner is more ready to use than a locked one is.) The autoblock had at least three full double-turns of 6mm prussic cord (6 wrapped strands). The loop showed no signs of weld-abrasion or any telltale signs that indicated loss of control on rappel.

The autoblock belay backup was clipped to the top of the right leg loop of his harness. The closed loop was 20-inches of 6mm accessory cord. The loop had "memory" in it that showed that it had been hung on with full body weight for an extended period of time. This memory would be consistent with hanging hands-free to look for a placement for the bolt he wanted to add to the Honeycomb section.

The only system flaw we could find was that Jim's autoblock loop was clipped to his right leg loop. This is currently considered state-of-the-art because it makes it easy to unset the hitch by raising your leg high. But this configuration can be problematic in those rare instances when the backup knot is set and you unintentionally raise the right leg too high or if you lose your erect posture. There is no known history of accidents in this configuration, so it has received no press. But there are more and more stories emerging of near misses where climbers accidentally "bump" their backup knot into their friction device and trigger rapid descents. If there is one thing worse than not having a backup knot behind your rappel device, it is having a backup knot you depend on that might fail.

Injuries

1) Jim had a few bloody (pre-mortem) abrasions on his right posterior shoulder, elbow and thigh. This constellation of injuries is consistent with a low speed slide presumably at the start of his fall.

2) Important negatives: he had no rope burns on his hands or anywhere else. We can infer from this that he did not lose control while rappelling. He had no high-speed abrasions that would have indicated he hit or slid on the rock face during the fall.

3) Jim had a classic constellation of injuries that were consistent with landing hard on his feet. These include a vertically oriented basal skull fracture

and a bloodless tibia/fibula fracture. The skull fracture would have caused immediate death upon impact.

4) Jim's body also showed blunt force trauma, mostly to his back and the back of his head, indicating that he fell backwards after landing on his feet.

Probable scenarios

1) Many climbers use an autoblock to get into hands-free mode. Jim may have been locked off while exploring where and how to place a bolt to protect the roof move in this climb. Lifting his leg to move or bumping his leg upwards in a fall could have rendered his autoblock ineffective. A bump of his autoblock would have caused a quick descent, which may not have been recoverable so close to the end of the rope.

2) As he neared the bottom of the rappel, he had to pendulum out to bounce onto the ledge under the overhang. Even if he landed on that ledge, the nature of the landing tends to pull you back out to a position that causes you to teeter on the edge. If he had successfully landed on the ledge and had raised his right leg, his autoblock could have crept up and hit his Reverso, triggering a rapid descent. This could have happened just as he was landing on that ledge. He would have been near or at the end of his rope (and in this case, a single strand at that point), so the sudden descent would not have been recoverable.

If he did this over the large flake (noted as "flake" on photo) below the west end of that lower ledge, he could have fallen a few feet, received the low speed abrasions on his right posterior side, and then fallen further out from the cliff.

There are a few other possible scenarios that we feel are significantly less probable than these two.

Coroner's finding

Jim died instantly from a basal skull fracture secondary to landing hard and upright on his feet. The spine drove upward into the skull, causing immediate death. His tibia/fibula fracture was bloodless, indicating that his heart had stopped immediately. He had other head trauma that occurred as he fell backwards immediately after this incident, but it was the basal skull fracture from the hard landing that killed him instantly. He also had low speed abrasions with a little blood on his right posterior shoulder, arm, and right leg.

It should be noted that the medical examiner could find no indication of a major medical event that might have contributed to this incident. There were no signs of any toxicity.

These negative autopsy results do not rule out the many possible medical complications that would not be detectable but could have easily contributed to this accident. For instance, when the coroner was asked about a dizziness episode Jim had complained about a month or so prior to his accident, the coroner responded that dizziness could easily have been from a cardiac ar- rhythmia or some other similar medical episode that could have triggered his fall but would have been undetectable by the forensic pathologist during the autopsy. This is a possible scenario, but there is no reason to think this is the probable scenario.

(NB: There are medical complications not detected by an autopsy. Some of these medical problems are truly undetectable while others would only be detected if specifically looked for.)

Tests conducted

Jim Richards and John Kanengieter re-rigged Jim Ratz's rope. Jim Richards then rappelled on it. When he got to the lower ledge, he only had two feet of rope to spare on each end. This means that Jim's rope, with uneven ends, would have run out of one strand of the dual rappel rope even sooner.

There was a two-bolt belay anchor installed at this ledge, above the ledge and ten feet to the right. For Jim to get to that anchor, he would have to move to the right, requiring even more rope.

The human factor

Jim Ratz co-owned Jackson Hole Mountain Guides. He was vice president of the board of trustees of the American Mountain Guides Association (AMGA). He was a former executive director of the National Outdoor Leadership School (NOLS) from 1984–1995. Jim had climbed and taught climbing since 1970. He was also a caver and had rappelled on static lines in pits over 1,000 feet deep. Jim was known to be a cautious and fastidious climber.

Local climbers and other guides who climbed with Jim say he was meticu- lous and thorough. He routinely checked and rechecked knots and systems. Jim displayed the careful habits expected of professional mountain guides. However, he may have been depending on a redundant safety system that occasionally doesn't work.

Jim may have made a serious error in judgment that we will never know about. While we cannot speculate as to Jim's state of mind at the time, we raise this point only because it is hard for us to conceive that with Jim's years of experience and level of skill that he would make a serious error in judgment during such a straight forward procedure that he had performed thousands of times in many settings and frequently on this particular route. It serves notice to all of us in the climbing community of the potential danger of losing concentration during familiar, routine tasks, as none of us is immune from being in a similar situation.

Recommendations

We recommend that the climbing community educate people about the problems associated with backup knots on leg loops and train people to make brake devices and backup knots coaxial. While this scenario is not definitive in Jim's case, the increasing incidences of near misses are clear predictors that we should pay attention to.

An alternative rig that avoids this problem is attaching your friction device to your harness with a single sling to put the device further from your harness. Then attach the backup knot on the belay loop on the harness in a way that it backs up your brake hand. This makes both devices co-axial. By attaching the device and backup knot at similar places on your harness, it becomes very difficult, if not impossible, to bump your backup knot into your friction device. (See the diagram of this published in the Petzl catalog at Petzl_122_123.jpg, which shows this coaxial arrangement.)

It can be said that tying the ends of the rappel ropes together would have prevented rappelling off the end. However, this climbing area has many vertical cracks left and right of the route (see photograph of the climb) and experienced climbers here have expressed great concern with having a knotted end caught in a crack. The result of this could prevent one from moving up or down, especially when doing roped solo climbing laps (an accepted form of climbing that has been done with very few incidents over the years), because minimal gear would be available for self-rescue. But this case clearly illuminates the fact that choosing to not use a backup knot in the end of a rope should not be taken lightly.

We recommend that the National Institute of Justice develop a national level coroner's form for recreational climbing fatalities. This is specifically because recreational climbing fatalities are so infrequent that local coroners need more guidance in preserving evidence at the scene. (Sources: Lead Investigator, John Gookin, Wyoming Deputy Coroner, SAR Commander with the Fremont County Sheriff's Office and the Curriculum Manager at the National Outdoor Leadership School [NOLS]; Tom Hargis, an AMGA certified guide for Exum Guide Service in other locations, a frequent climbing partner of Jim's who knew his habits and who bolted Honeycomb, so has knowledge of both the climb and the climber intimately; Jed Williamson, Managing Editor of this journal since 1974, and frequent investigator of accidents in a range of outdoor pursuits. John Gookin visited the site six times post-accident, Tom Hargis visited the site three times, and Jed Williamson visited the site once, with Gookin and Hargis. Williamson had numerous follow-up conversations and other exchanges with both.)

FALLING ROCK—DISLODGED BY PARTY ABOVE
Wyoming, Devil's Tower National Monument, Pseudo Weissner

On May 29, Rita Sanders (46) of Bellview, Nebraska, was injured by a falling rock while climbing on Devils Tower. Sanders was climbing the Pseudo

Weissner route with a friend and a professional guide when the accident occurred. She was preparing to climb the third pitch of the route and was attached to a set of anchor bolts when a 10- to 12-inch diameter rock was dislodged by a party climbing approximately 300 feet above her. The rock struck her in the helmet, left arm and left ankle, causing multiple injuries, including several broken bones. Sander's guide provided initial care and was lowered with Sanders 200 feet to the base of the route by another climbing party. Rangers and other climbers then packaged and lowered her in a litter through another 100 feet of vertical terrain. Sanders was then flown by the Rapid City Regional Lifeflight helicopter to Rapid City, South Dakota. (Source: Scott Brown, Chief Ranger)

Analysis
Climbing on the Devil's Tower brings with it an inherent risk these days. It would have been easy to add "poor position" as one of the contributory causes here, but that's the point. It's hard NOT to be in the fall-line here. Nevertheless, climbers must take even greater care to avoid causing rocks to fall. This is as important a skill to learn as all other climbing techniques. (Source: Jed Williamson)

FALL ON ROCK
Wyoming, Grand Tetons, Cloudveil Dome
On July 1, about 0630, Heather Paul (34) and Susie Schenk (38) departed from Lupine Meadows with plans to complete a traverse of Cloudveil Dome from the South Fork of Garnet Canyon. When they arrived at the Meadows of Garnet Canyon, because of ambient conditions they re-considered their plans to traverse Cloudveil Dome and instead decided that they would climb the South Teton. Since the ascent of the South Teton was essentially non-technical, they decided to stash their gear (rope and technical climbing equipment) at Garnet Meadows. They put on their mountaineering boots and then proceeded into the South Fork of Garnet Canyon.

When they arrived at a location below Cloudveil Dome in the South Fork of Garnet Canyon, they decided to complete the traverse of Cloudveil Dome after all, and ascended the Zorro Couloir route (which is actually on Spalding Peak to the west of Cloudveil Dome) to gain access to a col to the west of Cloudveil Dome. The ascent was essentially a snow climb and the condition of the snow was "soft, but not too soft—great for kicking steps." They arrived at the summit of Cloudveil Dome around 1230.

They then proceeded to scope out and down-climb the East Ridge Route of Cloudveil Dome in order to complete the traverse and return to the South Fork of Garnet Canyon. On a previous occasion, Heather had descended the East Ridge Route, which involved low 5th-class climbing, unroped. Susie was concerned because they had left their climbing gear and rope below in the Garnet Canyon Meadows. They decided to continue down the East Ridge Route with the alternative of ascending back to the summit of Cloudveil Dome and re-tracing their steps back down the Zorro Couloir in the event that they became uncomfortable with the East Ridge down-climb.

They were very comfortable down-climbing the East Ridge until they came to the second set of rappel anchors. (The first and second set of rappel anchors are sometimes used to descend the route using ropes when route conditions are poor, and/or by less experienced climbers.) The route-finding and down-climbing "got a little bit tricky." They were scoping out the route: Susie was checking down and to the right and Heather down and to the left. Heather told Susie that "this way looked good—doable—good handholds." Heather had good handholds, a good right-foot placement, and appeared to be fishing with her left foot for a foot-hold when she suddenly popped off and slid down a V-shaped corner. She hit a ledge feet-first a short distance down and plummeted off backwards (perhaps due to the weight of her backpack) down to a snowfield and out of sight. She was wearing a climbing helmet.

A significant SAR operation ensued, involving about 25 National Park rangers and Forest Service heli-tack crewmembers. One team of rangers climbed to Susie, who was in distress, and assisted her to a heli-spot where she was flown to the Lupine Meadows SAR Cache. Another group of rangers climbed to Heather's location and, after determining that she was deceased, flew her to the Lupine Meadows SAR Cache, where she was transported to Jackson.

Analysis

Heather Paul was an avid climber, mountaineer, skier, and world-class athlete. Why this tragic event ever happened and whether a similar event could be prevented in the future merits discussion.

When the two women left from the Lupine Meadows parking area early that morning, they planned on a west-to-east traverse of Cloudveil Dome. When they arrived at the Meadows of Garnet Canyon, they had a change of mind because of conditions, stashed their rope and technical climbing gear, and headed for the non-technical South Teton. Shortly thereafter, as they approached Cloudveil Dome, they had another change of mind and decided to attempt their original itinerary (but without the rope and technical climbing gear).

Did this indecisiveness contribute to the final outcome? Given the fact that mountaineering is not a static event, their change of plans based on existing environmental conditions demonstrated experience and knowledge of the mountain environment. Mountaineers should set a goal and define a specific itinerary to accomplish that goal, but they should also be willing to dynamically adjust to the environmental conditions that present themselves. Their decision to climb the South Teton and then to climb Cloudveil Dome via the Zorro Couloir as they originally had planned reflected changing environmental conditions and sound judgment.

Did stashing their technical gear and rope, and then proceeding with their original climb, contribute to the final outcome? When Heather and Susie arrived at the base of Cloudveil Dome, specifically the start of the Zorro Couloir, they encountered ideal snow conditions: the snow "was soft, but not too soft, great for kicking steps." Under these conditions, the placement of technical gear and use of ropes most likely was not necessary. Most climbers with their level of expertise probably would not have taken the equipment and rope from their pack. To the contrary, use of the gear and rope on the Zorro Couloir would probably have slowed them down considerably and subjected them to dangers such as falling rock and avalanche that often occur as the day progresses and ambient temperatures increase.

Did not having a rope on the descent of the East Ridge contribute to the final outcome? Heather and Susie were both highly competent mountaineers and well within their comfort level while descending the ridge. They also had a "fall-back plan" to re-trace their route and down-climb the Zorro Couloir should they become uncomfortable with their descent. Up to the moment when the accident occurred, they were comfortable with their descent. Although the route-finding had become "a bit tricky," consider Heather's last words: "This looks good—doable—good handholds." Under these circumstances, I doubt that the rope would have ever left their pack. Most climbers of their ability level, and even of lesser ability, down-climb the East Ridge route without a rope. Why? When mountaineers begin an ascent of a mountain, they do so with the understanding that there are many inherent risks involved that necessitate a balance between moving quickly through the mountains and doing it safely with the use of technical gear. (The use of ropes and gear may prevent a fall, but they slow your progress and expose you to falling rock and avalanche for greater periods of time.) If Heather and Susie had had a rope and had used it, certainly the tragic event would not have occurred; however, as noted above, I doubt that the rope would have ever left their pack and the outcome would have been the same.

Because of this, I see no flaw in Heather's and Susie's decisions throughout the day. They made these decisions based on a profound understanding of the mountain environment, balanced with their ability level. They were comfortable with their descent up to the moment of the accident. (Source: George Montopoli, Incident Commander)

ROCKFALL, UNFORTUNATE POSITION
Wyoming, Grand Teton National Park, The Snaz

On July 24, after a successful climb, our party of three was on the last (sizeable but sloping) ledge and final rappel of the route. I (Scott McGee, 39) was struck on the front half of my helmet by a bread-loaf-sized rock traveling at high velocity. I lost sensation and movement in my hands and feet, fell to my knees, and began to tumble backwards. (I experienced no loss of consciousness.) The first partner, who had just clipped in to rappel, arrested me by the harness and leg.

The second partner, a ski patroller, and I assessed potential injuries, ruling out destabilizing neck fracture and head injury. Normal sensation returned to feet and legs, but burning sensation persisted in hands. We elected to self-evacuate, stabilizing my neck, rappelling two short sections, and short roping to trail. Three miles travel on foot returned us to the trailhead.

Analysis

Although I was on a large ledge, I was not anchored. Anchoring until on rappel could have prevented the fall that my partner saved me from. The rockfall came with no warning or sound of tumbling from above. There was a party one pitch above, who reported neither hearing rockfall, nor knocking rocks off. The route is fairly steep (5.7-5.9 pitches), and the rock probably came from very high up.

CT and MRI revealed one bone spur chipped off of the front of C3 and no other damage to bone or soft tissue. Burning and tingling in arms diminished over two to three weeks and were caused in part by a pre-existing condition known as cervical stenosis, or bone spurring on the vertebrae, which narrows foramen, openings in the spinal column where nerve roots leave the spinal cord. These openings were likely pinched momentarily when the rock struck.

This rock could have easily missed me, hit elsewhere with a worse outcome, or struck me fatally had I been in a slightly different position. Wearing a helmet doubtless saved my life. Anchoring, even on large ledges, is something I'll consider more carefully in the future. In the meantime, I pursued surgery (fusion of C4-C7) as a preventative measure to keep major trauma to the neck from resulting in major disability. (Source: Scott McGee)

FALL ON ROCK, INADEQAUTE PROTECTION—ANCHORING ERROR, INEXPERIENCE
Wyoming, Hoback Junction, Rodeo Wall

On August 1, Sandy Edmiston (22) fell 60 feet to her death from the anchors of a bolted sport climb at the popular Rodeo Wall, south of Jackson. A novice climber, Sandy had learned to clean bolted anchors earlier that afternoon. On two climbs prior to the accident, she had safely cleaned and lowered off with step-by-step instruction. On the day's final climb, she struggled to negotiate the crux and reached the top of the climb after sunset, though still before dark. Believing that Sandy had demonstrated an understanding of how to clean an anchor safely, her partner did not talk her through the process a third time. This time, Sandy neglected to pass the rope back through the rappel rings after cleaning the draws from the anchor. Believing that she was on belay, she asked for slack so as to be able to unclip from the anchors, and when she did so, fell to the ground. She suffered severe head trauma and died on the scene.

Analysis

This accident once again stresses the importance of exercising constant vigilance when cleaning anchors. Furthermore, the training of novices in such seemingly simple but high-consequence techniques should be undertaken only under ideal conditions and should be closely monitored until mastery is certain. Any variation from the system, such as Sandy's request for slack after being put back on belay, should be examined very seriously. In this accident, inexperience, fatigue, and impending darkness were all contributing factors. Eliminating any of these might have averted a tragic loss. (Source: The climber's partner)

(Editor's Note: The victim's partner remains anonymous here out of respect for the difficulty one has in processing such events. It should be understood by the reader that he also recognizes his part in this event.)

FALLING ROCK–DISLODGED BY CLIMBERS ABOVE
Wyoming, Mount Moran, CMC

August 6, Jerry Painter (49), of Idaho Falls, Idaho, and three other climbers were ascending the CMC Route—a popular climbing route on the east face of Mount Moran, rated 5.5—when Painter was struck on the head by a sizable rock that was dislodged by climbers above. The rock broke Painter's helmet and he sustained injuries to his head and neck. The party was on the first pitch of the climb and had reached an elevation of about 11,500 feet when the accident occurred. Steve Bohrer, also from Idaho Falls and one of Painter's climbing partners, called for help via cell phone at 9:15 a.m. Rangers immediately began to coordinate a rescue, while the group of climbers moved Painter to a more secure area, out of the way of further rockfall, until rangers could reach them. Due to the nature of Painter's injuries, his disoriented state of consciousness, and the group's remote location, rangers asked for an assist from the interagency helicopter. The helicopter flew four rangers to a staging area on the Falling Ice Glacier, then inserted one of these rangers to Painter's location using the short-haul method. This ranger loaded Painter into an evacuation suit and attended him while the two were short-hauled back to the staging area at the glacier. Rescue personnel at the glacier moved Painter inside the helicopter for the flight to Lupine Meadows, where a park ambulance was waiting to transport him to St. John's Medical Center in Jackson. From there, Painter was flown by air ambulance to Idaho Falls for treatment of his head injuries. While Painter sustained serious injuries, his use of a helmet, combined with a rapid evacuation, likely saved his life. (Source: From an NPS Morning Report)

FALL ON ROCK, OFF-ROUTE—LATE START LED TO HASTE
Wyoming, Grand Teton National Park, Lower Exum

On September 3, Leah Samberg fell 35 feet from the third pitch of the Lower Exum Ridge (5.7), shattering her upper left arm and breaking her hip.

Mid-morning that day, Samberg, a first-year leader, and partner Alex Hamlin had set out from the Meadows intending to climb the complete Exum Ridge (5.7). Good weather had blessed the Labor Day weekend with light winds and sunny skies, and the high peaks of Garnet Canyon were crowded with parties eager to capitalize on the perfect climbing weather.

By the time that Samberg and Hamlin reached the base of the route at 1100, parties were already descending the Owen-Spaulding, and the Lower Exum was clear. Though aware of their late start, the pair took heart from the many escape options afforded by the Lower Exum, and from their success two weeks earlier on Beyer's East Face (5.9) up the same peak. Keeping an eye on the weather, they soloed the fourth-class approach and the beginning of the first pitch before roping up.

Making quick progress through the first two pitches, the pair reached the large belay ledge at the base of the third pitch; at this point escape is possible via a ledge leading left into the gully west of the Exum Ridge. At this point Samberg took the lead, climbing the left of two crack systems on the ridge crest; the pair believed theirs to be the beginning of the route's 5.7 third pitch. Climbing easily through the cracks first 40 feet, she placed gear regularly before running it out 15 feet above a blue Alien cam.

At this point the crack system petered out, and for several minutes Samberg traversed left and right searching for the route, finding neither handhold nor gear placement. It was becoming clear that the pair had chosen the wrong crack system, and that the route lay 20 feet to their right.

It was then that Samberg slipped. Though anxious, Samberg had not been gripped or pumped. The fall was completely unexpected, simply the result of either a hand or foot popping off the rock at the wrong moment. She fell twenty feet before she first hit the rock, smashing her elbow into a slab. Bouncing off, she fell another 10 feet, bouncing off her hip before the rope came taught. The blue Alien had caught her fall.

Hamlin lowered Samberg to the ledge and inspected her for injuries. Conscious, breathing, and with no obvious bleeding, Samberg complained of the pain in her shoulder, and was unable to walk. She was, however, able to sit, and so Hamlin helped her onto the ground, dressing and covering her in their down jackets. Using a backpack pad, they fashioned a makeshift splint before setting about getting help.

With a broken arm and possibly fractured pelvis, they agreed that she would not be able to descend on her own. Though the pair did not have a cell phone, due to the low wind, Hamlin was able to shout to parties descending the Owen Spaulding route for help. Climbers in the vicinity of the black dike heard his shouts and ran to the Ranger station on the lower saddle where a rescue was launched.

Exum guide Ben Gilmore ran from the saddle with a sleeping bag and cell phone, while the rangers called for a helicopter. Gilmore reached the pair first, and helped make Samberg as comfortable as possible while they waited for the helicopter to arrive. About half an hour later, two Jenny Lake Rescue Rangers, Jack McConnell and Marty Vidak, were deposited by helicopter on the ledge at the end of a 100-foot rope, followed by a litter.

Samberg was back-boarded, placed in the litter, and then, with McConnell hanging beside her, was long-lined down to the saddle. After moving the litter inside the helicopter, she was transported to Lupine Meadows where an ambulance was waiting to bring her to the hospital in Jackson. The total time from fall to ambulance was around two to three hours.

Samberg would find that she had shattered her upper humerus into eight pieces, completely shearing the ball joint off. She also cracked her hip in two places, though the fracture was not displaced.

Analysis

Several factors contributed to this accident. Both climbers were fit, capable at grades more difficult than the Lower Exum, and comfortable with climbing at altitude on the Grand; Samberg's runout likely resulted from a false sense of security. Though not extraordinary by alpine rock standards, Samberg's 15-foot runout resulted in a serious 35-foot fall on less-than-vertical terrain. Had her blue Alien not held, it is likely that she would have decked, with far more serious consequences.

In addition, the pair's late start had engendered a sense of urgency that likely contributed to the pair rushing their route-finding. Though Hamlin and Samberg had considered both crack systems and consulted the topo and route description, it's possible that with more time the pair would not have gotten off-route.

Finally, though strong technical climbers, the pair had only a handful of years experience in the high mountains on which to base their decision making. Though mistakes in route finding are inevitable, a willingness to turn around and reconsider one's decisions is a critical asset in the mountains, and one that comes mainly from experience. (Source: Alex Hamlin)

(Editor's Note: Chris Harder was the Incident Commander on the rescue, and he later interviewed Leah Samberg in the hospital. Her analysis, reflected in Hamlin's report, and Harder's conclusions are basically the same. It is always better to go with first-hand accounts.)

STATISTICAL TABLES

TABLE I
REPORTED MOUNTAINEERING ACCIDENTS

	Number of Accidents Reported		Total Persons Involved		Injured		Fatalities	
	USA	CAN	USA	CAN	USA	CAN	USA	CAN
1951	15		22		11		3	
1952	31		35		17		13	
1953	24		27		12		12	
1954	31		41		31		8	
1955	34		39		28		6	
1956	46		72		54		13	
1957	45		53		28		18	
1958	32		39		23		11	
1959	42	2	56	2	31	0	19	2
1960	47	4	64	12	37	8	19	4
1961	49	9	61	14	45	10	14	4
1962	71	1	90	1	64	0	19	1
1963	68	11	79	12	47	10	19	2
1964	53	11	65	16	44	10	14	3
1965	72	0	90	0	59	0	21	0
1966	67	7	80	9	52	6	16	3
1967	74	10	110	14	63	7	33	5
1968	70	13	87	19	43	12	27	5
1969	94	11	125	17	66	9	29	2
1970	129	11	174	11	88	5	15	5
1971	110	17	138	29	76	11	31	7
1972	141	29	184	42	98	17	49	13
1973	108	6	131	6	85	4	36	2
1974	96	7	177	50	75	1	26	5
1975	78	7	158	22	66	8	19	2
1976	137	16	303	31	210	9	53	6
1977	121	30	277	49	106	21	32	11
1978	118	17	221	19	85	6	42	10
1979	100	36	137	54	83	17	40	19
1980	191	29	295	85	124	26	33	8
1981	97	43	223	119	80	39	39	6
1982	140	48	305	126	120	43	24	14
1983	187	29	442	76	169	26	37	7
1984	182	26	459	63	174	15	26	6
1985	195	27	403	62	190	22	17	3
1986	203	31	406	80	182	25	37	14

	Number of Accidents Reported		Total Persons Involved		Injured		Fatalities	
	USA	CAN	USA	CAN	USA	CAN	USA	CAN
1987	192	25	377	79	140	23	32	9
1988	156	18	288	44	155	18	24	4
1989	141	18	272	36	124	11	17	9
1990	136	25	245	50	125	24	24	4
1991	169	20	302	66	147	11	18	6
1992	175	17	351	45	144	11	43	6
1993	132	27	274	50	121	17	21	1
1994	158	25	335	58	131	25	27	5
1995	168	24	353	50	134	18	37	7
1996	139	28	261	59	100	16	31	6
1997	158	35	323	87	148	24	31	13
1998	138	24	281	55	138	18	20	1
1999	123	29	248	69	91	20	17	10
2000	150	23	301	36	121	23	24	7
2001	150	22	276	47	138	14	16	2
2002	139	27	295	29	105	23	34	6
2003	118	29	231	32	105	22	18	6
2004	160	35	311	30	140	16	35	14
2005	111	19	176	41	85	14	34	7
TOTALS	6,111	958	11,098	2003	5,158	715	1,373	292

TABLE II

Geographical Districts	1951–2004			2005		
	Number of Accidents	Deaths	Total Persons Involved	Number of Accidents	Deaths	Total Persons Involved
CANADA						
Alberta	514	142	1033	6	0	10
British Columbia	307	114	641	10	5	16
Yukon Territory	35	27	77	2	1	10
New Brunswick	1	0	0	0	0	0
Ontario	37	9	67	0	0	0
Quebec	31	10	63	0	0	0
East Arctic	8	2	21	0	0	0
West Arctic	1	1	2	1	1	5
Practice Cliffs[1]	20	2	36	0	0	0
UNITED STATES						
Alaska	472	175	803	8	3	15
Arizona, Nevada Texas	84	17	153	3	1	6
Atlantic–North	914	145	1599	19	1	35
Atlantic–South	93	23	166	3	1	6
California	1215	284	2478	28	6	48
Central	133	16	215	0	0	0
Colorado	722	200	2255	18	8	22
Montana, Idaho South Dakota	78	31	124	0	0	0
Oregon	191	105	440	4	2	4
Utah, New Mexico	157	57	289	2	1	4
Washington	1012	310	851	16	7	46
Wyoming	536	123	984	10	4	24

[1]This category includes bouldering, artificial climbing walls, buildings, and so forth. These are also added to the count of each province, but not to the total count, though that error has been made in previous years. The Practice Cliffs category has been removed from the U.S. data.

TABLE III

	1951–04 USA	1959–04 CAN.	2005 USA	2005 CAN.
Terrain				
Rock	4237	521	73	7
Snow	2235	346	33	7
Ice	249	158	5	0
River	14	3	0	0
Unknown	22	9	0	1
Ascent or Descent				
Ascent	2853	578	61	9
Descent	2192	362	48	9
Unknown	248	12	2	1
Other[N.B.]	7	0		
Immediate Cause				
Fall or slip on rock	2958	283	49	7
Slip on snow or ice	950	207	21	11
Falling rock, ice, or object	601	135	9	2
Exceeding abilities	525	30	10	2
Illness[1]	362	26	13	0
Stranded	323	52	6	1
Avalanche	278	125	6	2
Exposure	264	13	1	1
Rappel Failure/Error[2]	263	45	11	2
Loss of control/glissade	192	16	7	1
Nut/chock pulled out	191	9	5	0
Failure to follow route	171	29	5	1
Fall into crevasse/moat	153	50	0	0
Piton/ice screw pulled out	94	12	1	1
Faulty use of crampons	92	5	3	1
Lightning	46	7	0	0
Skiing[3]	51	11	2	0
Ascending too fast	64	0	1	0
Equipment failure	14	3	0	0
Other[4]	385	35	28	2
Unknown	61	9	0	1
Contributory Causes				
Climbing unroped	979	163	8	2
Exceeding abilities	881	200	4	2
Placed no/inadequate protection	673	96	26	0
Inadequate equipment/clothing	651	68	13	2
Weather	452	64	10	3
Climbing alone	383	69	6	2
No hard hat	316	29	11	1

	1951–04 USA	1959–04 CAN	2005 USA	2005 CAN
Contributory Causes (continued)				
Nut/chock pulled out	196	32	3	0
Inadequate belay	190	28	7	0
Poor position	157	20	9	0
Darkness	136	20	4	1
Party separated	113	12	2	0
Failure to test holds	93	31	4	1
Piton/ice screw pulled out	86	13	0	0
Failed to follow directions	71	11	2	1
Exposure	57	13	2	3
Illness[1]	39	9	1	0
Equipment failure	11	7	0	0
Other[4]	256	100	0	0
Age of Individuals				
Under 15	125	12	1	0
15–20	1235	203	8	0
21–25	1337	251	21	6
26–30	1235	208	22	3
31–35	1029	112	22	2
36–50	1148	138	29	5
Over 50	206	29	11	2
Unknown	1933	517	40	13
Experience Level				
None/Little	1724	299	15	5
Moderate (1 to 3 years)	1544	354	31	0
Experienced	1797	433	58	7
Unknown	1958	535	25	24
Month of Year				
January	209	25	9	0
February	198	55	4	0
March	292	68	7	0
April	389	38	8	1
May	865	57	17	5
June	1009	69	17	1
July	1085	250	24	4
August	1002	181	9	3
September	1147	74	8	1
October	435	38	4	4
November	180	16	4	4
December	93	24	0	0
Unknown	17	1	0	0
Type of Injury/Illness (Data since 1984)				
Fracture	1116	216	55	7
Laceration	657	71	13	0

	1951–04 USA	1959–04 CAN	2005 USA	2005 CAN
Type of Injury/Illness (Data since 1984) (continued)				
Abrasion	309	76	12	0
Bruise	433	81	17	2
Sprain/strain	305	31	9	2
Concussion	214	28	10	0
Hypothermia	147	16	5	0
Frostbite	116	9	4	3
Dislocation	109	16	4	0
Puncture	43	13	0	0
Acute Mountain Sickness	40	0	2	0
HAPE	66	0	2	0
HACE	23	0	1	0
Other[5]	294	47	8	2
None	207	188	17	0

N.B. Some accidents happen when climbers are at the top or bottom of a route, not climbing. They may be setting up a belay or rappel or are just not anchored when they fall. (This category created in 2001. We still have "Unknown" because of solo climbers.)

[1]These illnesses/injuries, which led directly or indirectly to the accident, included: exhaustion (9); dehydration; hypothermia; hypoxia; AMS; HAPE; HACE; frostbite; dislocation; fractured ankle; back strain—prior condition.

[2]These include: inadequate anchors (8); rappelled off the end of the rope (2); inattention by belayer when lowering.

[3]This category was set up originally for ski mountaineering. Backcountry touring or snowshoeing incidents—even if one gets avalanched—are not in the data.

[4]These include: unable to self-arrest (7); hand or foot hold broke off (5); pulled on stuck rope after rappel—lost balance and fell; miscommunication (4); late starts resulting in haste or darkness (3); failure to recognize signs and symptoms of AMS/HAPE; no spotter—bouldering (3); off route, rock dislodged by party above (2); slack in rope on glacier travel—crampons caught; misuse of Grigri; poor decision making—underestimated slope conditions and did not dig test snow pit.
[5]These included: dehydration and exhaustion (3); collapsed lung (2); tension pneumothorax (2); ruptured spleen; tooth—incisor split by falling rock.

(Editor's Note: Under the category "other," many of the particular items will have been recorded under a general category. For example, the climber who dislodges a rock that falls on another climber would be coded as Falling Rock/Object, or the climber who has a hand-hold come loose and falls would also be coded as Fall On Rock.)

MOUNTAIN RESCUE UNITS IN NORTH AMERICA
**Denotes team fully certified—Technical Rock,
Snow & Ice, Wilderness Search;
S, R, SI = certified partially in Search, Rock, and/or Snow & Ice

ALASKA
Alaska Mountain Rescue Group. PO Box 241102, Anchorage,
AK 99524. www.amrg.org
Denali National Park SAR. PO Box 588, Talkeetna, AK 99676.
Dena_talkeetna@nps.gov
US Army Alaskan Warfare Training Center. #2900 501 Second St., APO AP 96508

ARIZONA
Apache Rescue Team. PO Box 100, St. Johns, AZ 85936
Arizona Department Of Public Safety Air Rescue. Phoenix, Flagstaff, Tucson,
Kingman, AZ
Arizona Division Of Emergency Services. Phoenix, AZ
Grand Canyon National Park Rescue Team. PO Box 129, Grand Canyon, AZ 86023
**Central Arizona Mountain Rescue Team/Maricopa County Sheriff's Office
MR.** PO Box 4004 Phoenix, AZ 85030. www.mcsomr.org
Sedona Fire District Special Operations Rescue Team. 2860 Southwest Dr.,
Sedona, AZ 86336. ropes@sedona.net
Southern Arizona Rescue Assn/Pima County Sheriff's Office. PO Box 12892,
Tucson, AZ 85732. http://hambox.theriver.com/sarci/sara01.html

CALIFORNIA
Altadena Mountain Rescue Team. 780 E. Altadena Dr., Altadena, CA 91001
www.altadenasheriffs.org/rescue/amrt.html
Bay Area Mountain Rescue Team. PO Box 19184, Stanford, CA 94309 bamru@
hooked.net
California Office of Emergency Services. 2800 Meadowview Rd., Sacramento, CA.
95832. warning.center@oes.ca.gov
China Lake Mountain Rescue Group. PO Box 2037, Ridgecrest, CA 93556
www.clmrg.org
Inyo County Sheriff's Posse SAR. PO Box 982, Bishop, CA 93514 inyocosar@
juno.com
Joshua Tree National Park SAR. 74485 National Monument Drive,
Twenty Nine Palms, CA 92277. patrick suddath@nps.gov
Los Padres SAR Team. PO Box 6602, Santa Barbara, CA 93160-6602
Malibu Mountain Rescue Team. PO Box 222, Malibu, CA 90265.
www.mmrt.org
Montrose SAR Team. PO Box 404, Montrose, CA 91021
Riverside Mountain Rescue Unit. PO Box 5444, Riverside,
CA 92517. www.rmru.org rmru@bigfoot.com
San Bernardino County Sheriff's Cave Rescue Team. 655 E. Third St.
San Bernardino, CA 92415
www.sbsd-vfu.org/units/SAR/SAR203/sar203_1.htm
San Bernardino County So/ West Valley SAR. 13843 Peyton Dr., Chino Hills, CA
91709.

San Diego Mountain Rescue Team. PO Box 81602, San Diego, CA 92138. www.sdmrt.org

San Dimas Mountain Rescue Team. PO Box 35, San Dimas, CA 91773

Santa Clarita Valley SAR / L.A.S.O. 23740 Magic Mountain Parkway, Valencia, CA 91355. http://members.tripod.com/scvrescue/

Sequoia-Kings Canyon National Park Rescue Team. Three Rivers, CA 93271

Sierra Madre SAR. PO Box 24, Sierra Madre, CA 91025. www.mra.org/smsrt.html

Ventura County SAR. 2101 E. Olson Rd, Thousand Oaks, CA 91362 www.vcsar.org

Yosemite National Park Rescue Team. PO Box 577-SAR, Yosemite National Park, CA 95389

COLORADO

Alpine Rescue Team. PO Box 934, Evergreen, CO 80439 www.heart-beat-of-evergreen.com/alpine/alpine.html

Colorado Ground SAR. 2391 Ash St, Denver, CO 80222 www.coloradowingcap.org/CGSART/Default.htm

Crested Butte SAR. PO Box 485, Crested Butte, CO 81224

Douglas County Search And Rescue. PO Box 1102, Castle Rock, CO 80104. www.dcsarco.org info@dcsarco.org

El Paso County SAR. 3950 Interpark Dr, Colorado Springs, CO 80907-9028. www.epcsar.org

Eldorado Canyon State Park. PO Box B, Eldorado Springs, CO 80025

Grand County SAR. Box 172, Winter Park, CO 80482

Larimer County SAR. 1303 N. Shields St., Fort Collins, CO 80524. www.fortnet. org/LCSAR/ lcsar@co.larimer.co.us

Mountain Rescue Aspen. 630 W. Main St, Aspen, CO 81611 www.mountainrescueaspen.org

Park County SAR, CO. PO Box 721, Fairplay, CO 80440

Rocky Mountain National Park Rescue Team. Estes Park, CO 80517

Rocky Mountain Rescue Group. PO Box Y, Boulder, CO 80306 www.colorado.edu/StudentGroups/rmrg/ rmrg@colorado.edu

Routt County SAR. PO Box 772837, Steamboat Springs, CO 80477 RCSAR@co.routt.co.us

Summit County Rescue Group. PO Box 1794, Breckenridge, CO 80424

Vail Mountain Rescue Group. PO Box 1597, Vail, CO 81658 http://sites.netscape.net/vailmra/homepage vmrg@vail.net

Western State College Mountain Rescue Team. Western State College Union, Gunnison, CO 81231. org_mrt@western.edu

IDAHO

Bonneville County SAR. 605 N. Capital Ave, Idaho Falls, ID 83402 www.srv.net/~jrcase/bcsar.html

Idaho Mountain SAR. PO Box 741, Boise, ID 83701. www.imsaru.org rsksearch@aol.com

MAINE

Acadia National Park SAR. Bar Harbor, Maine

MARYLAND
Maryland Sar Group. 5434 Vantage Point Road, Columbia, MD 21044
Peter_McCabe@Ed.gov

MONTANA
Glacier National Park SAR. PO Box 423, Glacier National Park,
West Glacier, MT 59936

Northwest Montana Regional SAR Assn. c/o Flat County SO,
800 S. Main, Kalispell, MT 59901

Western Montana Mountain Rescue Team. University of Montana,
University Center—Rm 105 Missoula, MT 59812

NEVADA
Las Vegas Metro PD SAR. 4810 Las Vegas Blvd., South Las Vegas,
NV 89119. www.lvmpdsar.com

NEW MEXICO
Albuquerque Mountain Rescue Council. PO Box 53396, Albuquerque,
NM 87153. www.abq.com/amrc/ albrescu@swcp.com

NEW HAMPSHIRE
Appalachian Mountain Club. Pinkham Notch Camp, Gorham, NH 03581

Mountain Rescue Service. PO Box 494, North Conway, NH 03860

NEW YORK
76 SAR. 243 Old Quarry Rd., Feura Bush, NY 12067

Mohonk Preserve Rangers. PO Box 715, New Paltz, NY 12561

NY State Forest Rangers. 50 Wolf Rd., Room 440C, Albany, NY 12233

OREGON
Corvallis Mountain Rescue Unit. PO Box 116, Corvallis, OR 97339
www.cmrv.peak.org

(S, R) **Deschutes County SAR.** 63333 West Highway 20, Bend, OR 97701

Eugene Mountain Rescue. PO Box 20, Eugene, OR 97440

Hood River Crag Rats Rescue Team. 2880 Thomsen Rd., Hood River,
OR 97031

Portland Mountain Rescue. PO Box 5391, Portland, OR 97228
www.pmru.org info@pmru.org

PENNSYLVANNIA
Allegheny Mountain Rescue Group. c/o Mercy Hospital,
1400 Locust, Pittsburgh, PA 15219. www.asrc.net/amrg

Wilderness Emergency Strike Team. 11 North Duke Street, Lancaster,
PA 17602. www.west610.org

UTAH
Davis County Sheriff's SAR. PO Box 800, Farmington, UT 84025
www.dcsar.org

Rocky Mountain Rescue Dogs. 3353 S. Main #122, Salt Lake City, UT 84115

Salt Lake County Sheriff's SAR. 3510 South 700 West, Salt Lake City, UT 84119

San Juan County Emergency Services. PO Box 9, Monticello, UT 84539

**Utah County Sherrif's SAR. PO Box 330, Provo, UT 84603. ucsar@utah.uswest.net

**Weber County Sheriff's Mountain Rescue. 745 Nancy Dr, Ogden, UT 84403. http://planet.weber.edu/mru

Zion National Park SAR. Springdale, UT 84767

VERMONT

**Stowe Hazardous Terrain Evacuation. P.O. Box 291, Stowe, VT 05672 www.stowevt.org/htt/

VIRGINIA

Air Force Rescue Coordination Center. Suite 101, 205 Dodd Building, Langley AFB, VA 23665. www2.acc.af.mil/afrcc/airforce.rescue@usa.net

WASHINGTON STATE

**Bellingham Mountain Rescue Council. PO Box 292, Bellingham, WA 98225

**Central Washington Mountain Rescue Council. PO Box 2663, Yakima, WA 98907. www.nwinfo.net/~cwmr/ cwmr@nwinfo.net

**Everett Mountain Rescue Unit, Inc. 5506 Old Machias Road, Snohomish, WA 98290-5574. emrui@aol.com

Mount Rainier National Park Rescue Team. Longmire, WA 98397

North Cascades National Park Rescue Team. 728 Ranger Station Rd, Marblemount, WA 98267

**Olympic Mountain Rescue. PO Box 4244, Bremerton, WA 98312 www.olympicmountainrescue.org information@olympicmountainrescue.org

Olympic National Park Rescue Team. 600 Park Ave, Port Angeles, WA 98362

**Seattle Mountain Rescue. PO Box 67, Seattle, WA 98111 www.eskimo.com/~pc22/SMR/smr.html

**Skagit Mountain Rescue. PO Box 2, Mt. Vernon, WA 98273

**Tacoma Mountain Rescue. PO Box 696, Tacoma, WA 98401 www.tmru.org

North Country Volcano Rescue Team. 404 S. Parcel Ave, Yacolt, WA 98675 www.northcountryems.org/vrt/index.html

WASHINGTON, DC

National Park Service, EMS/SAR Division. Washington, DC

US Park Police Aviation. Washington, DC

WYOMING

Grand Teton National Park Rescue Team. PO Box 67, Moose, WY 83012

Park County SAR, WY. Park County SO, 1131 11th, Cody, WY 82412

CANADA

North Shore Rescue Team. 147 E. 14th St, North Vancouver, B.C., Canada V7L 2N4

**Rocky Mountain House SAR. Box 1888, Rocky Mountain House, Alberta, Canada T0M 1T0

MOUNTAIN RESCUE ASSOCIATION

PO Box 880868
San Diego, CA 92168-0868
www.mra.org • www.mountainrescuehonorguard.org

Monty Bell, President/CEO
San Diego Mountain Rescue Team, CA
ubs@att/net
619-884-9456
Term expires June 2006

Fran Sharp, Vice President
Tacoma Mountain Rescue Unit, WA
thegirlpilot@hotmail.com
360-482-6190
Term expires June 2006

Dan Land, Secretary-Treasurer/CFO
San Dimas Search and Rescue, CA
kayley@kayley.net
Term expires June 2006

Neil Van Dyke, Officer/Member at Large
Stowe Hazardous Terrain Evacuation Team, VT
neilvd@stoweagle.com
Term expires June 2007

Tim Kovacs, Public Affairs Director/PIO, Past President
Central AZ Mountain Rescue/Maricopa County SO MR, AZ
tkovacs@cox.net
602-819-4066

Charley Shimanski, Education Director/Office Member at Large
Alpine Rescue Team, CO
shimanski@speedtrail.net
303-384-0110 x11
Term expires June 2006

Dr. Ken Zafren, MD, FACEP, Medical Chair
Alaska Mountain Rescue Group, AK
zafren@alaska.net

Monty Bell, Immediate Past President